Praise for *Uncover Exciting History*

"Amy Puetz always finds the 'story' to tell about her person or event in history." Dr. Ruth Beechick

"How did a pirate help Americans win the Battle of New Orleans? How did a conscientious objector capture 132 Germans? Who developed a code language that was never broken during WWII?

"Story-telling is the greatest way to excite people about history, and Amy Puetz loves to tell stories. With vocabulary suited to middle grade children, the whole family will enjoy *Uncover Exciting History* as they gather 'round for family reading time. Each six-page story closes with Digging Deeper, a selection of discussion questions and project ideas to personalize the story. Period photos and maps enhance the book even more. *Uncover Exciting History* is a great resource for Christian families and those who yearn to see God's hand behind American history."

Marcia Washburn
Building Tomorrow's Generation at
marciawashburn.com

"*Uncover Exciting History* is light reading on a remarkable theme: the people and events who made America, never forgetting the God who made America's people and events. I punctuated my reading by hunting down family and regaling them with 'Did you knows?' This is history to whet the appetites of the whole family."

Rachel Starr Thomson
Author of *Tales of the Heartily Homeschooled*
& The Seventh World Trilogy

"Amy Puetz has a gift for history. Avoiding the dryness of excessive detail, Amy brings out the essence of other times and distant places, taking us along on the journey to meet famous generals, intrepid explorers, and common, everyday people who made their mark on our world. This collection of sketches isn't meant to be an in-depth study of world history. Instead, you'll find the collection a great way to introduce the reluctant historian in your family to the excitement and drama of the past. Short enough to be read easily and quickly, yet informative enough to give your kids a good overview of historical events, these narratives are the perfect way to whet your children's appetites for learning about history. Even better, they're written from a Christian perspective, giving your children an appreciation for God's providential hand in world history. Highly recommended!" Jonathan Lewis
Home School Enrichment Magazine

"I had the opportunity to review the book *Uncover Exciting History: Revealing America's Christian Heritage* and would like to share my findings with you. This book is an excellent introduction to many of the very important events that have occurred in America's history. I love that it comes from a Christian perspective leaving me the opportunity to use it as a read aloud, or hand it off to my older student for independent use. The short chapters are great as is, yet can easily become a spring board for older students (or moms planning a study) to do some research on their own. Best of all the chapters leave you wanting to know even more about each person, place in history, or event . . . isn't that what we are trying to evoke in our children, a love of learning with a desire to learn constantly?! If you'll be studying American History anytime soon, I suggest you pick up this wonderful resource." Niki
www.Handsofachild.com

Uncover Exciting History

Uncover Exciting History

By Amy Puetz

Revealing America's Christian Heritage
in Short, Easy-to-Read Nuggets

Published by A to Z Designs
Wright, Wyoming

The information in this book was originally published in the *Home School Enrichment Magazine.*
http://homeschoolenrichment.com/

Published by A to Z Designs
P.O. Box 429; Wright, WY 82732
www.AmyPuetz.com

Cover Design – Amy Puetz
Layout Design – Amy Puetz
Photographs – Library of Congress

ISBN 978-0-9825199-0-5

LCCN: 2009934084

Library of Congress Cataloging-in-Publication Data

Includes index.
I. 1. United States History—Christopher Columbus—1451-1506. 2. United States History—Colonial period—ca. 1587-1775. 3. United States—History—Revolutionary War. 4. United States History—Revival. 5. West (U.S.)—Expansion. 6. United States History—Wars. 7. United States History—Great Depression. 8. Christian Heritage & Providence.
II. Title

*To my Lord and Savior, Jesus Christ,
who is the true author of history.*

*To my amazing parents, Mike and Phyllis, who have
encouraged and supported me on the rocky road of life.
Words cannot express how much I appreciate you both!*

Contents

Bonus Chapters

Chapter 1

Christ-Bearer
Christopher Columbus

Christopher Columbus was born in 1451. As a boy growing up in Genoa, Italy, Columbus had two dreams: one was to sail the untamed seas, and the other was to live up to his name and be a Christ-Bearer.

When Columbus grew up, he developed a plan for reaching the Indies by sailing west. Unsuccessfully, he sought financial help from the king of Portugal. Columbus next headed to Spain, hoping that Ferdinand and Isabella might support him. Christopher anticipated that his intent of proclaiming the Catholic religion to the heathen in the Indies would appeal to the staunch Catholic monarchs of Spain. Although they were interested, they were busy fighting a war against the Moors.

Columbus waited. Many years he waited, until finally, in 1492, Ferdinand and Isabella agreed to finance Columbus's voyage across the Ocean Sea (Atlantic) to "the Indies," a general term used to describe the Far East including China, Japan, and India. Christopher's years of idleness were over—now he was going to do the work for which he had been born.

1

On August 3, 1492, at the age of forty-one, Christopher Columbus began his voyage to discover the Indies with ninety men and three ships—the *Niña, Pinta,* and *Santa Maria.* The fleet spent over a month in the Canary Islands acquiring provisions and having the rudder on the *Pinta* repaired. Finally they sailed west.

With each passing day, the sailors' fears increased. The notion that people thought the world was flat is a fabricated story started by Washington Irving in his book, *History of the Life and Voyages of Christopher Columbus.* In his log, Columbus never mentions the sailors being afraid of falling off a flat earth. Instead, they dreaded running out of provisions or being unable to return to Spain since the current was pushing them out to the unknown, and they resented being led by a foreigner. There is no historical evidence that they believed in a flat earth. Columbus never gave in to the crew's desires to turn back. He knew he would find the Indies.

One night, as Christopher walked the deck of the *Santa Maria,* he thought he saw a light in the distance. It was land! The next day, on October 12, 1492, Columbus set foot on an island he christened *San Salvador* (Holy Savior). Columbus praised God for allowing him to reach the Indies. He did not know that he had discovered a new land.

Sailing from island to island, Christopher claimed them for Spain. Toward the end of October he discovered the island of Cuba and thought it must be Japan. (He later changed his mind and thought Hispaniola was Japan.)

Columbus found it hard to explain in words the loveliness of the islands. They were so majestic and beautiful. Regrettably, he only found small amounts of gold. The natives willingly traded what gold they had for the hawk bells, beads, mirrors, and other little trinkets the Spaniards gave them. Columbus had promised to bring back gold, but how could he if he did not discover a mine?

Continuing the journey, Christopher next found an island that he named *la Isla Española* (Spanish Isle). Today it is called Hispaniola.

On Christmas Eve, the crew of the *Santa Maria* left the steering of the ship to a young boy, and unexpectedly the ship went aground on a coral reef. Columbus accepted the accident as Divine Providence because now the crew would have to establish a fort, and the men who stayed behind could find gold and have it ready when Columbus returned. He called the settlement *Navidad* (Nativity) because it was established on Christmas. On January 4, 1493, Columbus and his men set sail for Spain, which they reached in March, 1493. On their return, Columbus, who was called "Admiral of the Ocean Sea," was received as a hero.

CHRISTOPHER COLUMBUS

Christopher Columbus's second voyage had the makings of being an even greater success than his first. He sailed with seventeen ships, twelve hundred men, and priests to help the Christ-Bearer convert the heathen.

Arriving at Hispaniola in late November of 1493, they found Navidad burned to the ground and learned that the men had been killed by a neighboring tribe. Columbus built another fort—calling it *Isabela* in honor of the queen—but the location was infested with mosquitoes, and soon men were sick with malaria. Although Columbus was an amazing explorer, he was a very poor governor and was completely incapable of keeping his men in order. Leaving some men at Hispaniola, he went exploring, and when he returned to Isabela he found the situation worse. There were also four supply ships from Spain in need of cargo. Columbus was troubled. What could he send back? They had not found a gold mine yet, so he sent five hundred Indians as slaves.

Affairs in Hispaniola were going so badly that Ferdinand and Isabella sent for Christopher. Departing for Spain in 1496, Columbus was a humbled man. He felt these difficulties had come upon him because he had displayed so much pride on the success of his first voyage. To remedy this problem, he began dressing as a monk by wearing a simple brown robe with a knotted rope as a belt. His second voyage, however, had not been a complete failure because of the discovery of many new islands.

Columbus's third voyage began in 1498. His intent was to find the mainland of China and claim it for Spain. On July 31, a pleasant island with three majestic mountains came into view, which Columbus named *Trinidad* (Trinity). A few days later, the Spaniards set foot on the continent of South America. They found four fresh rivers flowing into the sea. Could they have found the Garden of Eden? They thought they had.

Suffering from arthritis, Columbus went to Santo Domingo, the new fort on Hispaniola, for a rest. The Spaniards on Hispaniola were still very rebellious, and in the summer of 1500, a new Chief Justice named Bobadill arrived. When he landed, he saw seven dead Spaniards Columbus had hanged. Quickly Bobadill had Columbus arrested, put in chains, and sent to Spain. The skipper of the ship offered to release him, but Columbus refused, wishing to be freed by the monarchs. When Ferdinand and Isabella learned of Columbus being in chains, they ordered his liberation at once, informing him that they had never ordered Bobadilla to imprison him. The Admiral of the Ocean Sea was no longer a great hero.

In 1502, Columbus embarked on his fourth and last voyage. Having great hopes for this trip, he called it "High Voyage." He planned to sail around the world. There were many storms on this journey. It is reported that once, during a particularly bad storm, Christopher read the account of Jesus calming the sea, then drew his sword from its scabbard and made the sign of a cross in the air, and miraculously the weather calmed.

Columbus was tired and wanted to return to Spain, but his four ships were so worm-eaten that they only made it to an island called Jamaica. They were marooned for one year. Although the natives were friendly, they became tired of feeding Columbus and his men. Knowing when there was going to be an eclipse, Christopher told them that unless they fed his men, he would block out the moon. Columbus's plan worked.

Finally help arrived, and Columbus was able to start back for Spain. He arrived on November 7, 1504. His fourth voyage had accomplished nothing.

Columbus believed till his dying day that he had found the Indies. The impact of what he had discovered was not recognized during his lifetime. Sincerely, Christopher tried to do right and be a Christ-Bearer, but sadly, many times he

5

failed. With diligence and optimism, he answered God's calling to go into the unknown. Even during his years of rejection and ridicule, he still pushed on with bold determination. He died on May 20, 1506, a remarkable man who had tried to live up to his name: Christ-Bearer.

Digging Deeper

What did Columbus think he had discovered?

How many voyages did Columbus make?

Who were the king and queen that supported his voyages?

Read *The World of Columbus and Sons* by Genevieve Foster. This book does an excellent job of giving an overview of world events during Columbus's life.

To learn more about the flat-earth error, read *Inventing the Flat Earth: Columbus and Modern Historians* by Jeffrey Burton Russell

Look on a globe and find Genoa, Cuba, Trinidad, Jamaica, and Hispaniola. (This last contains the countries of the Dominican Republic and Haiti).

Build a miniature replica of the *Santa Maria*. Purchase a model kit from your local hobby store or go online to www.model-ships.com.

Chapter 2

Settling the New World

If a new continent was discovered today, would our country be the first to stake a claim? Of course, there are no new continents waiting to be settled—but it's interesting to think how we would respond if there were. When looking into the reasons why Europe colonized the New World, three things stand out as the most significant: wealth, power, and religion. The spirit of adventure was also alive and well in those who first came to the Americas. Many people also looked at the New World as a place to make a fresh start.

Quest for Wealth

Since the discovery of America, the lure of riches seemed to sing a sweet song that carried from the shores of America to the great cities of Europe. Stories of great wealth were told by Columbus, the conquistadors, and other explorers. In Peru, the king tried to bribe the Spaniards with thousands of gold and silver plates from a temple, hoping they would leave his country. The plates were worth millions of dollars. It's no wonder that stories of the New World were exaggerated until people actually

7

believed that gold and silver were sitting on the ground in the Americas just waiting to be picked up by a lucky explorer or settler. The New World was rich! But to find these riches, a person had to be willing to work. Most treasure seekers wanted to make a lot of money quickly.

Spain and Portugal were masters of South and Central America, but other European countries made their presence known in North America. The English explorers John and Sebastian Cabot found rich fishing grounds in Newfoundland, and soon England and France had a handsome trade selling codfish.

Fur also became a very profitable trade. The Dutch in New Netherlands and the French in Canada traded cheap trinkets with the Indians for beautiful furs that brought in a nice profit when sold in Europe. Since the rivers of North America were teeming with valuable furs, going there seemed like finding the goose that laid golden eggs. In 1638, two Dutch ships arrived in Holland with the skins of 1,769 beavers, 314 otters, and 132 bears. Longing to tap into the abundant treasures of the New World, ambitious explorers and adventurers established settlements in the Americas.

Power

Surely the wealthiest nation would have the most power! Each European country longed to be a leading power. Since Spain had financed Columbus's voyages, they had control of Central America, the Gulf of Mexico, and much of South America. The wealth from the New World led to Spain's power.

England, France, Holland, and Sweden wanted a piece of the profitable pie too. Explorers were sent to America, and they claimed lands for their mother countries. Power-hungry countries fought in Europe and the Americas for the land in the New World. Whoever controlled trade in America would be very powerful. Spain was the undisputed master until their mighty Armada was destroyed by the

English in 1588. After that, other countries began settling in the New World as well.

Religion

Religion was also an important reason people colonized the New World. Strong desires to convert the natives to the Christian faith led to the establishment of colonies. From Catholic countries such as France and Spain, Jesuit priests were sent as missionaries to the New World. The Separatists of Plymouth and the Quakers of Pennsylvania shared the gospel with their Indian neighbors. Some of the less honorable explorers and settlers would kidnap Indians and send them to their homelands to be *Christianized.*

Dreaming of religious freedom, many people saw America as a haven where they could worship God as their faith dictated. All over Europe, religious wars were taking place—the Protestants against the Catholics and the Catholics against the Protestants. Whichever group had control would often mercilessly persecute the other.

During the Huguenot Wars in France, several hundred sturdy French Protestants began a settlement in Florida. The staunch Catholic Spaniards didn't relish the idea of heretics living in their land, and they annihilated the French. The Huguenots were not welcome in Canada, either. Perhaps if the industrious Huguenots had helped settle Canada, events might have happened differently, but as it was, only trappers and priests lived there. They did not want to make a permanent home; they were looking for wealth and adventure. A few French towns did grow, but nothing compared to the colonies in the New England area.

The Dutch began a colony they called New Netherlands. From the Indians they purchased Manhattan Island for twenty-four dollars. At their capital, New Amsterdam, a profitable fur trade was carried on with the Indians. Among those who settled in New Netherlands was a group of hard-working Protestants called the Walloons. These poor people had been driven from their homes along the Rhine and had sought refuge in Holland. In the New World, they were allowed to worship God freely.

One of Europe's most prominent rulers, Gustavus Adolphus, the Protestant king of Sweden, longed to start a colony in America. Perhaps in the New World there would be freedom of religion, he thought. The Thirty Years' War prevented him from carrying out his plan, but eventually a Swedish colony was started in 1638. More Swedes came and settled along the Delaware River.

The most well-known religious group that came to the New World was the Pilgrims. Other English colonies were established by people looking for religious freedom. In Massachusetts, the Puritans began a colony. William Penn helped establish a settlement in Pennsylvania for Quakers—a religious group that was persecuted by Protestants and Catholics alike. After the English Civil War (1642–51), many wealthy Royalists fled to Virginia where they built and lived on huge plantations.

Life in Europe
To fully understand why Europe colonized the New World, we must look at life in Europe at this time. During the 1500s and 1600s, wars were common and costly. Differing opinions about religion caused many bloody battles. Political conflicts often erupted between neighboring countries and power-hungry nations. These wars devastated crops, destroyed villages, and damaged the financial stability of the countries. People who were already poor became destitute. Unclean living conditions and ignorance often led to widespread sickness and plagues.

Life was hard for people of the lower classes, and for many, the New World offered a fresh start and a chance to be part of a budding nation. Opportunities for bettering oneself were very slim in Europe, but in the Americas hard work and determination would willingly be rewarded. The church and government also extracted large taxes from the populace in Europe. Protestants objected to paying taxes for the Catholic Church to use.

At first, only a few brave people left Europe, but soon they came in larger numbers. In 1630 there were fewer than five thousand colonists living in what became the thirteen colonies, but by 1730 there were over six hundred thousand. Those who were too poor to pay their own way offered to work as servants for a certain number of years if their voyage fare would be paid. These indentured servants were little more than slaves, but once their years of service were completed, they were free to own property. The ideals of starting a new nation and building a country inspired many groups to settle in America.

Slaves, Convicts, and Debtors

Not all the settlers in the New World were there by choice. Blacks from Africa were brought to America and sold as slaves. When England's jails became crowded, their convicts were sent to Virginia. The colony of Georgia was started by General James Oglethorpe, who arranged to empty the debtors' prison by sending them to the new colony.

Conclusion

From this diverse group of people—all with their own varied reasons for coming to America—our own country began. Each group brought new ideas with them, which when put together made up the United States of America. Their heritage is ours!

Digging Deeper

Name the countries that founded colonies in the New World.

What were the three main reasons Europe colonized America?

Imagine you live in a certain European country, and you have just learned that your family is going to a colony in the New World. Write a letter to a friend telling what you expect and why your family is moving.

This chapter was just an overview of a very broad subject. Those who want to know more would enjoy *Sweet Land of Liberty* by Charles C. Coffin. Originally published in 1881, this book has a biblical worldview and is very well-written.

Chapter 3

The Lost Colony of Roanoke

On April 26, 1587, a group of brave settlers departed from England to establish a colony in Virginia. Among the colonists were fourteen families, including eighty-seven men, seventeen women, and eleven children. The promised five hundred acres of free land were a welcome incentive to the men and women who joined the group. Their destination was Chesapeake Bay. Unfortunately, their Portuguese navigator and pilot, Simon Fernandez, took them to Roanoke Island instead.

Once Fernandez reached Roanoke he flatly refused to take them further, despite the orders he had received from Sir Walter Raleigh. By then it was July of 1587, and the settlers planned to remain at Roanoke until arrangements could be made to reach Chesapeake Bay.

What is commonly called "the Lost Colony" was not actually the first colony to inhabit Roanoke. In 1584, Raleigh sent Philip Amadas and Arthur Barlow to explore the new world and locate a place with a harbor that would be ideal for a colony. When Amadas and Barlow returned, they brought with them two Indians, Manteo and Wanchese, along with glowing reports of North America.

The land they investigated was named *Virginia* in honor of Queen Elizabeth, who was known as the virgin queen. Raleigh dreamed of taking a group of English men and women to the new land. From the queen he received a seven-year patent to establish a settlement in Virginia, but Raleigh himself did not guide it.

In 1585, the second voyage to Virginia began, this time to establish a long-term colony. Sir Richard Greenville and Ralph Lane led seven ships and five hundred men, many of whom were colonists. Ralph Lane served as governor. Regrettably, the Englishmen never tried to establish friendly relationships with the Indians. They brought the two captive Indians with them when they returned to Roanoke. While Manteo proved to be a good friend to the English, Wanchese remained loyal to his native tribe.

The trouble began with a silver cup stolen by the Indians. Lane sent Amadas and a group of soldiers to the neighboring village, and they burned the houses and crops.

Many similar events took place over the next few months. The king of Roanoke, Winginia, gathered together the neighboring tribes and plotted to annihilate the invaders. Learning of the plan, Lane decided to strike first. A night attack was organized—the soldiers were told to leave their shirttails out so they could recognize each other. In the following skirmish Winginia was slain, and the Indians were temporarily checked.

The situation might have escalated again if it had not been for the arrival of Sir Francis Drake in 1586. Supply ships were long overdue, and Drake offered to take the colonists back to England. Initially Lane and the settlers wished to remain, but when a dreadful hurricane hit Roanoke, they changed their minds. The storm seemed to Lane a judgment on them for their harsh treatment of the Indians. Lane and the colonists abandoned their fort and sailed with Drake. They arrived in England on July 27, 1586.

When the second colony arrived the following year, they began rebuilding the abandoned fort and houses left by Lane. Leading this group of men and women was John White, who had served as painter and scientific adviser for the first colony. This settlement was to be completely different from the previous attempt. Families had been selected instead of single men in the hopes that Roanoke would become a permanent home to the settlers. Among the colonists were Governor White's pregnant daughter, Eleanor Dare, and her husband, Ananias Dare.

All too soon, hostilities with the Indians resurfaced. One of the colonists, George Howe, went fishing and was later found dead. The English retaliated by attacking a group of Indians at night. As it turned out, the Indians belonged to Manteo's friendly tribe, the Croatans.

On August 18, 1587, Eleanor Dare gave birth to the first English child born in America. The governor's tiny grandbaby was christened Virginia in honor of her new home. About a week later, Margery Harvie also gave birth to a baby.

Supplies began running low, and it was decided that Governor White should go to England to get aid from Raleigh. White returned with Fernandez, and a small ship was left behind for the colonists. On August 27, 1587, White departed. He never saw his daughter and grandchild again.

White arrived in England at the worst time to obtain help. Quarrels between England and Spain had finally erupted into a war. Although White did manage to employ two small ships in 1588, the captains were more interested in privateering than in relieving the colony. The two ships were separated, and the rash captain of the *Brave*—the ship White sailed with—was foolish enough to attack a larger French ship. They limped back to England glad to still be alive. Again White waited. In 1588, the Spanish Armada attacked England. Every available ship was needed to defend Britain.

It was not until 1590 that White again sailed for Roanoke. The journey took longer than expected because, once more, the lure of rich prize ships laden with American goods from Spanish colonies was a great draw for the captains and sailors.

When White finally arrived at Roanoke, he found the fort deserted. On a tree near the fort were carved the letters CRO, and on a post of the fort was the word CROATAN. It had been prearranged that if the settlers moved during White's absence, they were to carve their whereabouts on a tree and place a cross above the word if there had been a conflict. There was no cross, so apparently the colonists had not experienced trouble. White had left behind three chests. These had been dug up, and the books, painting, and maps they contained were torn and damaged by rain. White and the captains planned to explore Croatan Island the following day, but a storm hit, which prevented any further investigation. On October 24, 1590, White was again in England. He never returned to Virginia, and it must have tormented him to remain in ignorance about the fate of his daughter and her child.

The Lost Colony of Roanoke is one of the great mysteries of history that is still open to speculation. What happened to the colonists? Why did they leave Roanoke? They may have gone to live with the Croatan Indians. As early as 1703, the Croatan Indians said they had white ancestors. Some think the colonists divided into two groups, one going to Croatan and the other settling somewhere in the Chesapeake Bay area.

When Jamestown was established, John Smith was told to find out what he could about the Lost Colony. Chief Powhatan told Smith the colonists had been massacred by his own men. Such news would have alarmed the feebly established colony at Jamestown, so Smith did not mention the news for some years.

There were other rumors too. Apparently a group of whites—two men, four boys, and a maid—were being held as slaves by the Indians. Smith and others never made any attempts to rescue them. One day, some men saw a yellow-haired Indian boy in the forest. He darted away before they could question him. Even if Powhatan had killed the settlers, these stories seem to indicate that some of the colonists may have survived and were living with the Indians, or perhaps these people were other whites who had been stranded.

Interest in the Lost Colony of Roanoke surfaced again in 1937, when some stones were found with names of the settlers carved on them. It seemed the mystery might be solved, but the stones turned out to be fakes. The fate of the Lost Colony many never be solved, but the sacrifices made by that settlement paved the way for future colonies to be established by England.

MAP OF ROANOKE BY JOHN WHITE

Digging Deeper

How did the Virginia colony get her name?

How many colonies were attempted at Roanoke?

How many men, women, and children were there in the Lost Colony?

Who was the first English baby born in Virginia? Who were the parents of the baby?

Pretend you are one of the colonists of the Lost Colony. Write a letter to your friends in England telling them what happened at Roanoke. Use your imagination. Create a dramatization if you prefer.

Make a time line of the events mentioned in this chapter.

Read *The Lost Colony of Roanoke* by Jean Fritz. This is a cleverly written, captivating account of the colony; it is also beautifully illustrated by Hudson Talbott.

Where is Roanoke located? The above book has a map.

To see a complete list of the names of the colonists as well as additional books go to www.AmyPuetz.com/Roanoke.html.

Chapter 4

The Pilgrims' Legacy

William Brewster's voice filled the cool October air as he said a benediction of thanksgiving to God Almighty. Around him, the other Pilgrims nodded their heads in heartfelt agreement; Chief Massasoit and the ninety Wampanoags Indians with him sat quietly in respect for the white man's God. With the prayer completed, the feasting began. The tables were heavily laden with delicious deer and wild turkey, nutritious vegetables, scrumptious pies, and various breads made from corn. Joyously, the celebrations continued for three days. There were foot races, wrestling matches, contests with guns, bows and arrows, and even a military drill led by Captain Standish. The Pilgrims' first Thanksgiving was truly a momentous celebration.

Who were these brave souls who had settled in a harsh wilderness, and what caused them to leave their homes in Europe? The Pilgrims belonged to a group of devoted Christians called Separatists. In England during the reign of King James I, there were two leading factions who opposed the Church of England. The Puritans were one group, thus called because they wanted to purify the Church from within. The other group was the Separatists, who completely broke away from the Church of England. The party of Separatists who later became the Pilgrims lived in the Midlands town of Scrooby, but because of religious persecution they fled to Leyden, Holland.

Although they enjoyed religious freedom in Holland, they found life very hard. They worked long hours, and they saw that it would be easy for their children to be lured into the sinful pleasures of the world. Prayerfully, they sought the will of God. He confirmed to them that they should begin a settlement in the New World. Lacking the financial means to attempt such an adventure, they borrowed money from a group of London Adventurers. The Adventurers were very corrupt, and in the end the Pilgrims paid an exorbitant amount.

Finally, in 1620, their journey began. Sailing first to England aboard their ship the *Speedwell*, they were joined by a larger vessel, the *Mayflower*. At Southampton, the "saints," as the Separatists called themselves, met the other settlers who were also traveling to the New World. Many of the "strangers," as the Separatists named them, proved sympathetic to the religious beliefs of the Separatists. Others were just looking for excitement.

On August 5, 1620, they set sail, only to turn back twice because the *Speedwell* proved leaky. Eventually, they continued with only the *Mayflower*. For sixty-six days they endured the tempest and fury of the Atlantic Ocean. They praised God when land was sighted. Before leaving the *Mayflower*, the saints and strangers drew up a document that was a binding agreement between them. The Mayflower Compact—which began with the words "In the name of God, Amen"—was the first document of self-government in North America. Bravely they faced the unknown with the knowledge that they and their children would be free to worship God as He was leading them.

The first winter in Plymouth Plantation was filled with many hardships, but the Pilgrims were always grateful for every blessing, whether small or great. Faithfully, God provided an ideal location for their town. Their charter was for land in Virginia, but heavy storms had prevented them from going south.

When they arrived in New England, they found an abandoned piece of land they named Plymouth in honor of the last English town they had sailed from. The ground had been cleared and was ready for planting. Before the Pilgrims arrived, this land had belonged to the Patuxet Indians. They had killed every white man who ventured into their territory. Then, oddly, a strange plague began among them, eventually destroying the entire tribe. Since the other tribes in the area saw how peculiarly the Patuxet had died, they avoided the region. Therefore, this piece of earth was uninhabited and belonged to no one. The Pilgrims gave thanks to God.

THE DEPARTURE OF THE PILGRIMS

21

During the first winter, the Pilgrims faced a devastating blow when nearly half their number died from sickness. The long months at sea with rotten food had weakened them. While scurvy claimed some lives, others died of pneumonia and consumption. Throughout the long winter, the healthy cared for the sick. There were days when only five men were well enough to care for the others. In the end, forty-seven of the original one hundred and two Pilgrims died. When spring began to appear, the Pilgrims prayed and hoped for a bright future.

The first spring began with a surprise. Walking boldly into Plymouth one day was an Indian. To their amazement, he spoke English. His name was Samoset, and he helped the Pilgrims make a treaty with Massasoit, their nearest neighbor. He also introduced them to Squanto, who proved to be a "special instrument" sent by God to help them.

Several years before, Squanto of the Patuxet tribe had been captured by a slave trader and taken to Europe where he learned English. He eventually escaped, but when he returned to his homeland, he discovered that his tribe and family had died of the plague. Strangely, Plymouth was built on the piece of land that had been his home. At once Squanto found himself drawn to the white men, and he deeply desired to help them.

If it had not been for Squanto, the Pilgrims might not have survived. Squanto taught them how to fish, plant corn, and fertilize the ground with fish. He interpreted for them with the Indians and helped them trade with various tribes. Indeed, he assisted the Pilgrims in learning the ways of their new home.

When fall emerged, the Pilgrims gathered a good harvest. Cheerfully, they celebrated a day of thanksgiving to God and invited the Indians to join in their merrymaking. The Pilgrims observed their first Thanksgiving!

Resourcefully, the Pilgrims prepared for the coming frost. They felt prepared for the winter until, one day in

November, 1621, the *Fortune* arrived with thirty-five colonists and only a few provisions. Before long, everyone was put on half rations. Starvation began to set in, and it appeared that this winter would be as bad as the first. Each person received only five kernels of corn a day, but by the miraculous hand of God, everyone survived the second winter.

The following summer they built houses and improved their living conditions. By the third summer, Governor William Bradford and the leaders began praying about how to produce a more abundant crop. Private property was the answer. Since landing, the Pilgrims had tried living in a communal setting, but it never provided enough food. Remarking on the venture of private property, Bradford said, "This was very successful." Never again were the Pilgrims in danger of starvation. In 1623, they gathered a bountiful harvest.

With so many blessings, the Pilgrims had a second Thanksgiving. Wishing to share their joy with others, they again invited the Indians. Massassoit arrived with his head wife, three other chiefs, and 120 braves. Before the feast began, everyone was served a dish with only five small kernels of corn, a reminder of how God had faithfully preserved them.

The Pilgrims were a group of righteous individuals who followed wholeheartedly after God. When confronted with persecution, they persevered with Christian virtue. Constantly, they sought the Lord's will and tried to faithfully follow it. Above all, they knew how to praise the Lord. When they experienced abundant blessings, they were thankful, and when suffering came they knew God would provide. May we find encouragement from their rich Christian legacy.

Digging Deeper

What religious group were the Pilgrims associated with?

List some of the reasons the Pilgrims settled in America.

On a map, find England and locate these towns: Southampton and Plymouth. Also find Leyden, Holland, and Plymouth, Massachusetts.

At your Thanksgiving dinner, place five kernels of corn by each place to remember the Pilgrims and the things they sacrificed for religious freedom.

Read *Of Plymouth Plantation* by William Bradford. This is an excellent book about the Pilgrims, their depth of character and Christian virtue. A wonderful book for children about the Pilgrims is *Three Young Pilgrims* by Cheryl Harness. This beautifully illustrated book lets you see the *Mayflower*, first winter, and Thanksgiving through the eyes of three historical Pilgrim children.

To learn more about Squanto's fascinating life, listen to *The Legend of Squanto* by Focus on the Family Radio Theatre.

Make a Pilgrim meal. *Eating the Plates, a Pilgrim Book of Food and Manners* by Lucille Recht Penner and *Food and Recipes of the Pilgrims* by George Erdosh are both excellent resources with Pilgrim recipes.

Chapter 5

The Great Awakening

The preacher's monotone voice echoed through the church in Northampton, Massachusetts. As the brilliant Jonathan Edwards spoke, he kept his eyes focused on the back wall of the church. Gently, Edwards's words began to sink into the hearts of the assembly, and although his method of speaking lacked enthusiasm, his words were powerful. Revival followed!

During the 1730s, the church in Northampton felt the stirring of the Holy Spirit, moving them from their lukewarm apathy to an awakening of their souls. Delivering his most famous sermon, "Sinners in the Hands of an Angry God," on July 8, 1741, in Enfield, Connecticut, Edwards helped spread the revival. A great commotion swept over the people, and they began wailing, crying, and screeching loudly. Frequently Edwards asked the congregation to control themselves so he might finish his sermon. As a result of his preaching and the work of the Spirit, lives began to change, and complete towns were transformed.

The event that has become known as the Great Awakening actually began years earlier in the 1720s. And, although the most significant years were from 1740–1742, the revival continued until the 1760s.

Many of the early colonists had come to the new world to enjoy religious freedom, but as the land became tamed and prosperous, they no longer relied on God for their daily bread. Wealth brought complacency toward God. As a result, church membership dropped. Wishing to make it easier to increase church attendance, the religious leaders had instituted the Halfway Covenant, which allowed membership without a public testimony of conversion. The churches were now attended largely by people who lacked a personal relationship with Jesus Christ. Sadly, many of the ministers themselves did not know Christ and therefore could not lead their flocks to the true Shepherd. Then, suddenly, the Spirit of God awoke as though from an intense slumber and began to touch the population of the colonies. People from all walks of life, from poor farmers to rich merchants, began experiencing renewal and rebirth.

The faith and prayers of the righteous leaders were the foundation of the Great Awakening. Before a meeting, George Whitefield would spend hours—and sometimes all night—bathing an event in prayer. Fervent church members kept the fires of revival going through their genuine petitions for God's intervention in the lives of their communities.

The early rays of the Great Awakening began with Theodore Frelinghuysen of the Dutch Reformed Church in New Jersey. Through his ministry, the hearts of his church members were changed. It was the young people who responded first and experienced the regeneration of becoming new creations. They in turn spread the message to their elders. Thus began the first spark of the Great Awakening.

There were many powerful preachers during this era. Among them was Gilbert Tennent. Years before, his father, William, brought his family from Ireland to New England because of religious persecution. Soon the elder Mr. Tennent and his family became members of the Presbyterian Church. Wanting his sons to join the ministry, he opened a college at Neshaminy, Pennsylvania. At the Log College (called that because it was built of logs), he taught his sons and other pupils Greek, Latin, and Hebrew. After college, Gilbert spread revival through New Jersey and Pennsylvania.

Other influential men helped expand the reach of the Great Awakening. Samuel Davies, a preacher and hymn writer (he penned "Great God of Wonders" and "Lord, I am Thine, Entirely Thine") carried the holy banner into Virginia. Bravely, David Brainerd preached to the Indians and settlers in the backwoods of Pennsylvania and New Jersey. Virginia and Georgia enjoyed the work of Daniel Marshall, and North Carolina was changed through the efforts of the Baptist preacher Shubal Stearns.

The most prominent theologian of the Great Awakening was Jonathan Edwards. Although not a powerful speaker, Edwards still managed to spread the revival. From his brilliant mind he constructed one of the most impressive sermons ever preached. He also wrote many books and pamphlets describing the events he saw in his own church.

The only son in a family of eleven children, Edwards was born on October 10, 1703. At the young age of thirteen he entered Yale (not unusual during this era of history), and he graduated in 1723. Four years later, Jonathan married the remarkable and virtuous Sarah Pierpont. Faithfully, Sarah helped Edwards in his ministry and personal endeavors.

In 1727, Edwards became the assistant minister at the Northampton church. When his grandfather, Solomon Stoddard, died, Jonathan became the minister and served in that church for nearly twenty-four years. He spoke boldly against the Halfway Covenant. Since many of the members who promoted the Halfway Covenant were merchants (or "river gods," as Edwards called them), they were able to make most of the decisions for the community, thus giving them the power over the rest of the populace. Edwards did much to help alleviate the tyrannical practices that followed.

While Edwards was the most prominent theologian of the time, by far the most influential and famous evangelist of the Great Awakening was George Whitefield. He was born in England and educated at Oxford, where he met and became friends with John and Charles Wesley. During his spare time at college, he visited the poor and those in prison. On June 20, 1736, at the age of twenty-two, he became an ordained minister. God blessed him with an amazing ministry, and wherever he spoke revival accompanied him.

At the Wesley brothers' request, Whitefield joined them in Georgia to continue his ministry. After a few months he returned to England and again reached thousands through his preaching. He became well-known in both the Colonies and Great Britain. His preaching spread revival and new birth to the hearts of those who listened.

Unfortunately, many ministers became jealous of his God-given ability. In Bristol, the churches refused to allow him the use of their buildings. Undeterred, Whitefield preached outside. On more than one occasion he addressed thirty thousand people. He spoke persuasively with a loud, commanding, and pleasant voice. With weighty emotion and dramatic power, Whitefield presented the gospel message to the masses, spreading the light of Christ with vigor and enthusiasm.

Whitefield also united the independent movements of the Great Awakening and bound the separate colonies into a unit. Breaking through denominational boundaries, he once said, "Father Abraham, whom have you in heaven? Any Episcopalians? *No!* Any Presbyterians? *No!* Any Independents or Methodist? *No, no, no!* Whom have you there, then Father Abraham? *We don't know those names here! All who are here are Christians—believers in Christ, men who have overcome by the blood of the Lamb and the word of his testimony.* Oh, is that the case? Then God help me, God help us all, to forget having names and to become Christians in deed and in truth!"

During his life, George Whitefield made seven tours of the colonies and preached eighteen thousand sermons! There was hardly a portion of the colonies that did not feel his influence and love.

The significant working of God during the Great Awakening was far-reaching. Truly converted members now filled the pews. In New England from 1740 to 1742, memberships increased from twenty-five thousand to fifty thousand. Hundreds of new churches were formed to accommodate the growth in churchgoers.

For the first time, the individual colonies had a commonality with the other colonies. They were joined under the banner of Christ. Clearly, their unity gave them strength to face the impending danger of war with England. Not only did the Great Awakening unite the colonies religiously, but also politically. After being freed from inner sin, the colonists also sought freedom from external tyrants. The motto of the Revolutionary War was, "No King but King Jesus!"

May God once again bring about a revival that will awaken our nation to our need for Him.

Digging Deeper

Who were the leading preachers of the Great Awakening?

What years did the revival take place?

Pretend you are at the church in Enfield the day Edwards preached his famous sermon, and write a letter to a friend or family member sharing your thoughts on the address.

Pray for revival. Prayer played an important part in the Great Awakening. As Jonathan Edwards said, "Prayer is as natural an expression of faith as breathing is of life." Now more than ever before, this country needs revival. Prayer is powerful and necessary for any revival.

Read the chapter "A Sunburst of Light" in *The Light and the Glory* by Peter Marshall and David Manuel.

Chapter 6

The French and Indian War
The Struggle for Mastery of North America

During the colonial era, wars between European nations often boiled over to include their colonies. The French and Indian War, or the Seven Years' War as it was called in Europe, was just such a conflict. Both New France and New England wanted to extend their boundaries in North America. The French wanted more territory to trap beavers and other furs, while the English planned to establish permanent settlements and farm the land. This often-overlooked war is perhaps one of the most influential conflicts in American history, because its outcome determined which nation would be master of North America.

Probably the most celebrated hero to emerge from the war was a young man in his twenties named George Washington. His exceptional qualities recommended him to Governor Dinwiddie of Virginia, who sent him as a messenger to the French in the Ohio Valley. In 1753, the French built a fort in this valley to keep the English from settling there.

Both of the mother countries claimed the Ohio Valley, and they were prepared to fight for it. Although the French

31

received Washington courteously, they had no intention of giving up *their* land. When the English realized the resolve of their rivals, they raised a regiment and planned to remove the French by force.

George Washington was assigned second in command of the hearty group of Americans and Indians. Traveling through the wilderness to the Ohio Valley, they captured a small group of French. After the French surrender, a serious tragedy occurred when Washington's Indian allies began butchering the defenseless French. Loud and furious were the reproaches hurled at Washington by the Frenchmen in North America for allowing such an outrage to occur.

On the return march to Virginia, Washington and his men built Fort Necessity in an attempt to temporarily fortify their position. Here, they faced an attack from a much larger group of French soldiers. Outnumbered, Washington accepted a truce which allowed him and his men to peacefully withdraw. Although Washington's initial taste of war had been a defeat, he still became a national hero.

THE DEATH OF GENERAL WOLFE

Even though war had not been formally declared, both England and France began sending troops to their colonies in North America. The Englishman chosen to lead the army into the Ohio Valley was General Edward Braddock, a conceited man who held the backwoodsman militia in contempt. Disregarding George Washington's advice, he marched his troops through the woods to attack Fort Duquesne as if they were in a parade. It was July 9, 1755. Suddenly, from behind every tree came a shower of bullets. The militia quickly adopted the Indian warfare techniques and hid behind trees, but Braddock scorned them as cowards. Confusion ensued as the British regulars poured a meaningless volley into the woods, trying to hit what seemed to them to be an invisible enemy.

Washington tried to regain order as bullets flew around him. The Indians fired at him specifically again and again, but God protected him, and Washington was the only one of General Braddock's aides who was not injured. Five horses were shot from under Braddock before he received a fatal wound. As he died, these words passed through his lips, "We will know better how to deal with them next time."

The English did eventually capture Fort Duquesne, and they renamed it Pittsburgh. However, Braddock's stubborn refusal to heed the advice of the American colonists in their first attempt to capture the fort had resulted in the death of five hundred English soldiers.

In 1756, the French and Indian War began in earnest. Most of the English military leaders were weak and incompetent. Brightly contrasting them was the French commander, Marquis de Montcalm, a brilliant leader who was full of resolve and quick thinking.

The fighting had now moved to Lake George, in present-day New York. At the top of the lake was the French held Fort Ticonderoga, and at the bottom was the English held Fort William Henry. Planning to capture Fort

William Henry, Montcalm made preparations for a decisive victory. When the English General Webb, commander of Fort Edward, learned of the intended attack, he sent only one thousand men to reinforce the fort and then, like a coward, stayed behind at Fort Edward.

Although General Webb was an irresolute man, the chief officer of Fort William Henry, Colonel Monro, was not. With only fifteen hundred men, Monro held the fort for six grueling days (August 3–9, 1757) against Montcalm and his army of eight thousand. A smallpox epidemic was raging inside the fort, and when their supplies were depleted, the brave Monro hung out the white flag. Defeat was inevitable, as Webb had refused to send reinforcements and provisions.

Montcalm admired bravery, and he offered generous terms to the defeated English, giving them safe conduct to Fort Edward if they wouldn't take up arms against the French for eighteen months.

As the conquered English marched solemnly from their staunchly defended fort, France's Indian allies suddenly attacked the unarmed English. The French did very little to stop the massacre, and nearly six hundred were killed. The bloody massacre at Fort William Henry enraged the English, and it lives as a sad chapter in American history.

England's numerous defeats in North America motivated Prime Minister William Pitt to action. Replacing the weak officers, he put Lord Howe in command of an expedition to capture the French-held Fort Ticonderoga. Lord Howe, a brave and able leader, appreciated the wisdom of those who lived in America. The army traveled by boat to the north end of Lake George and landed close to the fort. Boldly he led the attack! Before the English could taste the fruits of victory, however, their beloved leader was slain. The incompetent General Abercrombie took over the expedition and insisted on fighting in European fashion. Despite England's overwhelming numbers, Montcalm again gained a significant victory. The spiritless English general beat a hasty retreat and did not stop until he reached Albany, New York. Although New France demonstrated exceptional military leadership, it was completely dependent on the mother country for supplies.

One of the last battles of the French and Indian War was the capture of Quebec in 1759. The British sent General James Wolfe, a brave, capable, and enterprising man, to command this attack. Seated on lofty cliffs above the St. Lawrence River, the city of Quebec seemed an impregnable fortress. Many fortifications around the city made an attack seem impossible. General Wolfe had a plan, however, and on the night of September 12, 1759, he put his daring plan into action.

The English made a pretense of landing below the city, while Wolfe and his men actually landed above the city. At daybreak, ten thousand English soldiers stood before the city of Quebec on the Plains of Abraham. Montcalm had finally been outwitted!

The two brave commanders led their men into battle. In about fifteen minutes, the conflict ended. Both Wolfe and Montcalm were killed. However, before Wolfe expired, he learned that the French were defeated and said, "God be praised, I die in peace." This victory led to the fall of New France, although several scrimmages continued until the Treaty of Paris was signed on February 10, 1763.

The people who really experienced the most hardship as a result of the war were the Native Americans. During the conflict, Indian nations fought for their white friends. The Algonquians supported the French, and the Six Nations, consisting of the Iroquois, Mohawk, Seneca, Oneida, Cayuga, and Onondaga, sided with the English. Both England and France used their Indian allies to gain victories. But as the colonists expanded their borders, the Native Americans were pushed west. The Indian way of life inevitably changed.

With the conclusion of the French and Indian War, England became the powerful master of North America. Finally they had beaten their old rival, France. Despite England's fumbling commanders and disregard for the colonists, they had emerged triumphant.

Besides determining who would control North America, this war also gave many Americans training for a conflict they would soon be fighting against the mother country— the American Revolution. To pay for the French and Indian War, the British government began taxing the colonists, leading to the War for Independence. In His providence, God was preparing the men and the circumstances that would eventually lead to the formation of the United States of America.

Digging Deeper

Who were some of the leaders of the conflict?

When did hostilities begin?

When was the Treaty of Paris signed?

Read *Sweet Land of Liberty* by Charles C. Coffin. This is a reprint of a book written in 1881 and is the history of early explorations and the colonial era. If you wish to read just about the French and Indian War, start at chapter 31.

Another excellent book is *The Bulletproof George Washington* by David Barton, which tells the little-known story of Washington's Divine protection during the defeat of Braddock.

After reading the above resources, write a report about the French and Indian War.

Chapter 7

Freedom Founded

The Founding Fathers who signed the Declaration of Independence pledged their lives, fortunes, and sacred honor to the cause of freedom. Many of them suffered imprisonment and hardships for their oath to liberty. Others saw their homes pillaged and destroyed by the British. Some of their wives died from deprivation and anxiety.

Each one of the fifty-six men who signed the Declaration of Independence had ambitions and dreams. They were not just statesmen who met in Congress and discussed the subject of freedom; they were individuals who had families and homes. The signers tasted firsthand the horrors of war and the fury of the English. They were patriots and Christians! They were determined!

With an enormous amount of faith in Divine Providence, the Founding Fathers committed their cause to Almighty God before they affixed their noble names to the illustrious document that proclaimed liberty throughout the land. By learning about their lives, we get a glimpse into their freedom-loving hearts.

Edward Rutledge

Edward Rutledge of South Carolina was not only a signer but also a soldier. Leading a corps of artillery, he helped fight the British at the battle of Charleston in 1780. When the city fell into the hands of the English, Mr. Rutledge was made a prisoner. He was sent to St. Augustine, Florida, where he was held for about a year before he was exchanged. Experiencing the same fate of many soldiers during the Revolution, Mr. Rutledge knew the danger of taking up arms against the British nation. He promised his allegiance to America, and he never withdrew that pledge.

Richard Stockton

Richard Stockton of New Jersey paid for independence with his life. The Stocktons lived in a lovely colonial home in Princeton called "Morven." Intelligent people who understood the times would often be guests at Morven, where they received the Stocktons' generous hospitality. When the British under Cornwallis captured Princeton, Mrs. Annis Stockton did her country a great service by saving many state papers and the rolls and records of the American Whig Society of Princeton. The Stocktons fled to safety.

Later, Mr. Stockton was captured by a group of Tories and taken to a prison in New York where he received the most inhumane treatment. The horrors and anguish that so many prisoners of war suffered at the hands of the British during the Revolution were inflicted on Mr. Stockton with great severity because of his leadership among the people. At one time he was deprived of food for twenty-four hours. He was finally released, but it was too late; he had suffered much both physically and financially, as the British had demolished his property. The humiliation he endured when having to request assistance from friends to provide for his family was more than the good man could bear, and he died

38

in 1781. Perhaps the greatest legacy of his continual devotion to freedom was his dear wife, Annis, who wrote many patriotic poems during and after the Revolution. She promoted the independence which her husband had bought with his life.

Thomas Jefferson

Thomas Jefferson, perhaps a better-known signer, also suffered a great loss because of his act for freedom. Martha Jefferson, Thomas's beloved wife, was forced to flee from Richmond, Virginia, when the British occupied the town in 1779. Departing from the city with her baby in her arms, Martha and her children were taken to a place of safety about fourteen miles away. Although the British searched Monticello, they did not destroy it.

In April, 1781, the Jeffersons' baby died. The strain on Mrs. Jefferson was extreme. She was constantly anxious about her husband's safety and felt deeply the loss of their child. The next year she gave birth to another child, but this baby also died. Martha, who had never been strong, began slowly to sink into the grave.

Devotedly, Thomas cared for his wife during her illness. She died in September of 1782. Mr. Jefferson was devastated and would often go for long rambles through the woods to ease his grief. Had Mrs. Jefferson not been forced to escape from the enemy, and had she not had concern for her husband, it is possible that she might have lived many more years. Thomas Jefferson's price for liberty was the thing he loved most in the world: his wife.

John Hart

The price that John Hart paid for signing the Declaration of Independence was high. John Hart from New Jersey owned and cultivated a large estate. Being a devoted family man, John and his wife Deborah had twelve children whom they raised in the fear and admonition of the Lord.

After the signing of the great document for freedom, Mr. Hart and his family experienced the cruelty of the British. The first years of the war were devastating for America as they found themselves powerless to stop the onslaught of the English. When the British, accompanied by the Tories and Hessians, were in control of New Jersey, they violently destroyed Mr. Hart's estate. Mrs. Hart had been taken ill and was unable to travel a great distance, but her children managed to move her out of harm's way before the English arrived. Mr. Hart hurried to his family to see about their safety. Because of his involvement with the Declaration of Independence, he was a man with a price on his head. He was forced to depart from his wife's deathbed with the British hot on his heels.

Going from place to place, the loyal signer dared not stay two nights in the same place for fear of discovery and the danger it might bring upon those who harbored him. Despite his age and infirmities, he was hunted as a criminal until the American victory at the battle of Trenton. He was a ruined man. His many months of hiding as a fugitive had destroyed his health, his wife had died, and his estate had been pillaged. But he still clung to the ideals that he had declared to defend with his life, fortune, and sacred honor. When he passed away in 1780, he died a true patriot, a devout Christian, and a hero of freedom. John Hart, signer of the Declaration of Independence, paid for our liberty with all he had.

William Floyd

William Floyd of New York sacrificed his fortune for the cause of independence. After the Battle of Long Island, Mr. Floyd's estate fell into the hands of the enemy. His wife, Hannah, and children sought safety in Connecticut. Occupying his property, the British consumed his large herds of livestock and even used his house as a stable for their horses. For seven long years Mr. Floyd did not receive any profit from his own property. Sadly, Mr. Floyd also lost his wife, who had been unable to survive the misfortunes and misery she endured. The personal loss that William Floyd suffered did not deter his decision for emancipation. He was willing to pay the price!

Some of the signers did give their very lives for freedom. Many also gave their earthly fortunes—but not one sacrificed his sacred honor. Their sacred honor remained with them all the days of their lives. Laying the foundation for a country that the world had only dreamed of, they gave all they had for its establishment. We must keep alive their ideals and the liberty for which they died.

This Fourth of July, read the Declaration of Independence and reflect upon the men who made the document a reality. The signers' lives exemplified the words of Patrick Henry: "Is life so dear, or peace so sweet, as to be purchased at the price of chains and slavery? Forbid it, Almighty God! I know not what course others may take, but as for me, give me liberty or give me death!"

The signers chose independence and freedom was founded!

Quotes from the Founders

"(W)e will look for the permanency and stability of our new government to Him who bringeth princes to nothing and teacheth senators wisdom."
John Hart, signer of the Declaration of Independence

"(The) liberty to worship our Creator in the way we think most agreeable to His will (is) a liberty deemed in other countries incompatible with good government and yet proved by our experience to be its best support."
Thomas Jefferson, signer of the Declaration of Independence

"(T)hat the way of life held up in the Christian system is calculated for the most complete happiness that can be enjoyed in this mortal state."
Richard Stockton, signer of the Declaration of Independence

"We have this day restored the Sovereign, to Whom alone men ought to be obedient. He reigns in heaven and . . . from the rising to the setting sun, may His kingdom come." Samuel Adams, after signing the Declaration of Independence

"A patriot without religion in my estimation is as great a paradox as an honest man without the fear of God."
Abigail Adams, in a letter to Mercy Warren, 1775

"Religion and morality are the essential pillars of civil society."
George Washington

"God grant that in America true religion and civil liberty may be inseparable and that the unjust attempts to destroy the one may in the issue, tend to the support and establishment of both."
John Witherspoon, signer of the Declaration of Independence

Chapter 8

Crossing the Delaware
A Turning Point of the Revolution

It was Christmas day in 1776. The American soldiers in the Continental Army crowded around campfires, trying to shake off the chill of the bleak December day. A cloud of despair hung over the men. Missing their families, the soldiers felt the War for Independence was already lost. In the distance, the Delaware River floated by. It was the only thing between them and the English. Discouragement and despair seemed to envelope those in the fight for freedom in America. The men in George Washington's army never guessed they would soon be engaged in another battle— only this time they would be victorious.

The campaign of 1776 resulted in one defeat after another for the Continental Army. At New York they barely escaped complete annihilation, and from there they lost battles at White Plains and Fort Washington. As they retreated, the British pursued them like hounds chasing a fox. Miraculously, the fox in this case always managed to escape. Congress was disheartened by the progress of the war and began discussing replacing Washington with General Charles Lee. Lee was an ambitious, unreliable, and untrustworthy man, but before Lee was made commander in chief, the British captured him.

Washington knew his country and men needed a victory, and when Cornwallis made the mistake of stretching out his army, Washington knew he must act. Since Cornwallis needed the men to live off the land, he divided his force and garrisoned them at Bordentown, Burlington, Mount Holly, Princeton, and Trenton. Many of the American soldiers were nearly done serving their enlistment, and Washington knew he must proceed quickly—while he still had an army. He decided to attack the Hessian troops at Trenton. The Hessians were a German mercenary force, foreign soldiers employed by the British.

On Christmas Eve, Washington communicated the final plans to his generals. They would cross the Delaware River at three places and surprise the enemy. General John Cadwalader and Adjutant General Joseph Reed were to cross at Bristol with fifteen hundred men and attack Burlington. General James Ewing and seven hundred men were to hold the bridge at Assunpink Creek, which was at the end of Queen Street in Trenton. Leading the third part of the attack would be Washington himself. He, along with Generals Greene, Sullivan, and Stirling and twenty-four hundred soldiers of the Continental Army, would cross the Delaware at McKonkey's Ferry. Closer to Trenton, they would divide their force and attack the town from two sides. Operations would begin on Christmas Day, and if all went well they would reach Trenton at five o'clock on December 26, 1776.

As the disheartened Continental Army formed ranks, they were told the password with which they could distinguish friend from foe. It was "Victory or Death."

Each man received enough food for three days and sixty rounds of ammunition. Marching through a frigid rain, they arrived at McKonkey's Ferry around dusk. The Delaware River was higher than usual and congested with ice. Soon a storm was roaring. Although the squall helped cover their noise, it also slowed their progress.

While Henry Knox managed the crossing on the Pennsylvania side, Washington oversaw the troops as they landed on the New Jersey side. The passage was made in Durham boats, which had flat bottoms and high sides. In charge of the boats were Colonel John Glover and the experienced sailors from Marblehead, Massachusetts. (These sailors had come to Washington's aid before, when he and his men were cornered at Brooklyn. John Glover and his men helped them escape under cover of darkness.)

Since the boats were somewhere between forty to sixty feet long, nearly forty men could be transported at a time. Getting the horses and cannons loaded and across proved to be the most difficult part of the night. Finally, at three in the morning on December 26, 1776, all of Washington's army was on the New Jersey side. By now they were three hours behind schedule and could never reach Trenton before daybreak. Yet Washington was determined to advance!

The march to Trenton was treacherous. A furious storm with alternating rain, snow, sleet, and hail hindered every step, and a bitterly cold wind ripped at their faces. Many soldiers had only rags instead of shoes on their feet, and they suffered terribly. Along the march, two men froze to death. Of the three-pronged plan, only Washington was able to advance. The storm held the others back.

The commander of the Hessian troops at Trenton was Colonel Rall, who had displayed great valor and bravery at the battles of White Plains and Fort Washington. Although Colonel Rall received warning of the Americans' intended attack, he did not take them seriously. He even received a message from a Loyalist shortly before the battle, but he put it in his pocket unread. On Christmas Day, the Hessians celebrated the holiday in the flamboyant German fashion.

Despite the delays, the Continental Army was able to make a surprise attack. At approximately eight o'clock in the morning, the first fighting began when General Greene and his men met guards on the Pennington Road. The storm was blowing into the faces of the Hessians and gave the advancing Americans the advantage. In an orderly retreat, the Hessians made their way to Trenton.

The town of Trenton had two main roads going through it: King Street and Queen Street, which ran parallel to each other. By the time the startled Hessians assembled, Knox's artillery held positions at the heads of both King and Queen Streets. A grueling fight began. The element of surprise added to the confusion. The Hessians placed a field gun on King Street and might have done real damage to the Americans, but the patriots seized the gun and used it against the Hessians instead! Colonel Rall rallied his men who were enduring heavy fire. Under a shower of bullets, the Hessians retreated to an orchard southeast of town. After Colonel Rall was mortally wounded, the Hessians surrendered. In less than forty-five minutes the battle was over, and the jubilant Continental Army was victorious.

WASHINGTON CROSSING THE DELAWARE

Washington had won the day without the loss of one man in battle. Of the Hessians, twenty-one were killed, ninety were wounded, and over nine hundred were taken prisoner. Only five hundred Hessians escaped. Taking the baggage of the vanquished, the Americans added six cannons and one thousand muskets to their supplies.

The British were stunned when they learned of the American victory at Trenton. When Lord Cornwallis received the news, he was on the verge of sailing for England to see his sick wife. Instead, he journeyed back to New Jersey with the intent of defeating Washington and the rebels. Soon, all of the United States was praising Washington and his Continental Army for their glorious victory. Discouraged people began to hope that the war could be won, and Congress was happy to retain Washington as commander of the troops.

After the victory, the army marched back to McKonkey's Ferry again and recrossed the Delaware. Nearly a week later, Washington led a surprise attack on the British at Princeton. Again the Americans tasted the sweet fruit of victory.

The American triumph at Trenton was the turning point of the American Revolution. Having held the patriots in contempt, the British were now forced to respect them. In early December of 1776, the young nation had reached its lowest point. The war seemed hopeless and defeat inevitable, but the daring crossing of the Delaware and the subsequent victory at Trenton were a balm to the reeling and weak nation.

Convinced that Washington was the most able leader of the army, Congress wisely kept him in that capacity until the conflict ended. Many men now began to enlist, and filling the ranks was not difficult.

America suffered many other setbacks during the conflict with Great Britain, but never was the war in such a state of despair as it had been before Trenton. If the bold surprise had not been undertaken at such a critical time, it is quite possible that the United States of America might have lost the Revolutionary War.

Digging Deeper

Why was the Continental Army so discouraged in December of 1776?

Where did Washington cross the Delaware?

Who was the commander of the Hessian troops at Trenton?

How many Americans were killed during the battle of Trenton?

Read *The Boys of '76* by Charles C. Coffin. This book was written in the 1880s, and it is an excellent manuscript that gives a firsthand account of the American Revolution.

Find a map of Trenton during Washington's campaign (*The Revolutionary War* by Bart McDowell has a map on page 104, or go to this link: http://www.britishbattles.com/battle-trenton.htm). Draw the layout of the town on a large piece of paper; construction or art paper would work well. Using beans or toy soldiers, reenact the battle on the paper.

Chapter 9

The Making of a Republic
The Story of the Constitution

A group of stern-faced men gathered in Independence Hall. At the front of the room sat George Washington, on the back of his chair the image of a half-sun that the aged Benjamin Franklin studied thoughtfully. The closed windows made the room as warm as an oven, and the disagreements did not help any. It was the hottest summer anyone could remember.

Through perseverance and determination, these fifty-five men created the most incredible document of self-rule ever conceived by mankind. The story of how we ended up with "We the people" is a long and beautiful epic.

The government of the United States began when the American colonists declared their independence from Britain. Shortly after signing the Declaration of Independence, Congress wrote the Articles of Confederation, which bound the states together. During the Revolution, the common enemy the states faced gave them a bond that held them together. With the coming of peace in 1783, Congress, operating under the Confederation, realized how little power they had. When they needed money to pay their debts, they could only *ask* the states to

49

pay taxes—but most of the states disregarded their requests. Some states even sent diplomats to foreign countries as if they were their own separate nation. People viewed loyalty to their state as more important than national patriotism.

The 1780s have been called "the Critical Period" because of the anarchy that took place during that decade. An economic depression settled over the country after the Revolution. There was little hard money, and the paper money that was being printed was worthless. Laws were disrespected, and crime was rampant. In 1786, the unrest and despair of those years came to a head when Daniel Shay and a group of former soldiers took up arms in Massachusetts, and after burning farms, tried to capture an arsenal. The soldiers in Shay's Rebellion were angry that their farms were being seized because they could not pay their debts. When the state militia finally put down the rebellion, the states were forced to reevaluate their current form of government. Many Founding Fathers, among them George Washington, saw the need for a more unified country.

In 1786, many leaders attended a convention at Annapolis to discuss the problems facing the nation. Only five states sent delegates, so the leaders called for another convention to revise the Articles of Confederation. In May 1787, the delegates met in Philadelphia. Every state except Rhode Island sent men to represent it. Of the fifty-five men who attended, many had already dedicated their lives to their country. Eight of the men who had signed the Declaration of Independence were there, including Benjamin Franklin. Many wise men who urgently felt affairs could not continue as they were came to create a new form of government.

With a unanimous vote, George Washington was elected president of the convention. The very presence of the former Commander in Chief gave credibility to the gathering.

After the beginning procedures, the convention got down to business. On May 29, Edmund Randolph presented what became known as the Virginia Plan. In this plan, created by James Madison, a whole new form of government complete with three branches was proposed: the executive, legislative, and judicial. The Virginia Plan proposed a stronger central government.

Those who wanted to keep the Articles of Confederation came up with their own plan, and William Paterson of New Jersey presented it on June 15. The Paterson Plan wanted to preserve the equality of the small states by continuing the practice of each state having one vote regardless of population or size.

Fervently, the eloquent statesmen debated over the two plans. The large states insisted that more delegates should represent them than the small states. And the small states could not agree to a plan where they were not given an equal vote. Round and round they went. Many might have left and forgotten the whole thing—but there was Washington, with the same determined look that he had worn at Valley Forge. Who could walk out on a man like Washington?

During this debate, Franklin, who was suffering from gout and bladder stones, made a suggestion: "I have lived, Sir, a long time, and the longer I live, the more convincing proofs I see of this truth: 'that God governs in the affairs of man.' And if a sparrow cannot fall to the ground without His notice, is it probable that an empire can rise without His aid?" He concluded, "I therefore beg leave to move that, henceforth, prayers imploring the assistance of Heaven and its blessing on our deliberation be held in this assembly every morning before we proceed to business." After this, things began running smoother.

On July 5, Roger Sherman of Connecticut proposed the Great Compromise. Sherman was a devout Christian and a sensible Founding Father. During America's short and turbulent history, he had signed the Declaration of Independence, the Articles of Association, and the Articles of Confederation. He would soon sign the Constitution, the only man to have his signature appear on all four documents! His Compromise suggested separating Congress into two houses: one that was based on population and the other giving each state an equal voice. The storm that had nearly sunk the convention was over. The Great Compromise passed on July 16.

There were other smaller gales to pass through, and the month of August was spent debating the role of Congress, the office of president, and slavery, but all these were finally resolved to the satisfaction of the majority. On September 17, 1787, the Constitution was signed by thirty-nine of the forty-two delegates who were still there. Those who refused to sign felt uneasy because it lacked a Bill of Rights.

Now the Constitution was sent to the states to see if they would accept it. Only nine states were needed to ratify it. The delegates of the Constitutional Convention went home to encourage their states to approve the new form of government.

Patrick Henry, Samuel Adams, and many other Founding Fathers opposed the Constitution. Fearing that the states were giving up too much control, they thought there needed to be a Bill of Rights. To educate the people and explain how the new republic would work, James Madison, Alexander Hamilton, and John Jay wrote essays for the newspapers. Their writings were collected into a book and published under the title *The Federalist Papers*. Thus people who opposed the Constitution were called Anti-Federalist.

Delaware was the first state to ratify the Constitution on December 7, 1787, and other states followed. In the important states of New York and Virginia, heated debates were taking place. In Virginia, Madison was working hard to convince the state to sign, and in New York, Hamilton was just as vocal. Finally both states joined, but it was a close margin. In Virginia the votes were eighty-nine for and seventy-nine against, and in New York it was thirty to twenty-seven. These states were only pacified when they were promised that a Bill of Rights would be added.

True to their word, the first Congress created ten amendments to the Constitution: the Bill of Rights. With the news that the Constitution had been ratified, celebrations were held. They had reason to rejoice! The fact that the independent thirteen states had finally decided to become a nation was the Divine work of Providence.

When reading the Constitution, it is interesting to think about how the Founders created such a farsighted document. The roots of the Constitution first appeared when the Pilgrims penned the Mayflower Compact. Over one hundred years of colonial government gave the Founders a useful idea of what made a good government. The number one source the Founders relied on for guidance was the Bible. Among other legal works that inspired them were Blackstone's *Commentaries on the Law* and the writings of John Locke.

As the delegates were signing the new Constitution, Benjamin Franklin commented on the half-sun depicted on the back of Washington's chair. Throughout the long summer, he had wondered if the artist had meant to depict the sun as rising or setting. Now at the end of the convention, with success finally achieved, Franklin remarked, "Now at length I have the happiness to know that it is a rising, and not a setting sun." Little did those men know that day how brightly indeed the sun was rising!

Digging Deeper

What were the Articles of Confederation?

Who was the president of the convention?

Define the word "anarchy."

Make an outline of the events mentioned in this chapter.

Read *Shh! We're Writing the Constitution* by Jean Fritz. This short, illustrated book gives a basic overview of the Constitutional Convention.

Watch *A Spiritual Heritage Tour of the United States Capitol* by David Barton. In this captivating educational video, David Barton gives a tour of the Capitol. It's not expressly about the Constitution, but it is mentioned.

Chapter 10

To Kentucky and Beyond
America Begins the Push Westward

It is hard to imagine that places like Kentucky, Tennessee, and Ohio were once considered the West, but there was a time in American history when this was true. During the years between the French and Indian War and the American Revolution, the growing colonies began pushing their way toward the setting sun until they reached the Appalachian Mountains.

As more colonists came from various parts of Europe, many people felt crowded in the east. There were tales of a magnificent land west of the mountains, and soon the name of Kentucky set backwoodsmen to dreaming. Men like peddler John Finley, who had been to Kentucky, praised the land as abundant in furs and game. One man in particular enjoyed hearing Finley's stories of the western lands—his name was Daniel Boone. During the French and Indian War, John Finley and Boone had both driven wagons for General Braddock on his ill-fated march into the Ohio Valley.

Vividly, John Finley shared with Boone his knowledge of a pass through the mountains that was used by the Indians, which eventually became known as the

55

Cumberland Gap. The Indians in the south traveled through the Cumberland Gap when they journeyed on the Warrior's Path to make war on their enemies in the north. The stories of this magnificent country sparked Daniel Boone's imagination and he decided to see Kentucky for himself.

On the other side of the ocean reigned the king of England, George III, who thought that the American colonies were costing the government too much money. Besides the expense of the French and Indian War, English soldiers were needed to protect settlers from the Indians. King George devised the perfect solution to the problem, outlined in the Proclamation of 1763, which forbade settlements west of the Allegheny Mountains. If the colonists did not enter Indian lands, England would not have to send soldiers to protect them.

The hearty and energetic pioneers—in their typical independent fashion—felt their need for elbow room was more important than a proclamation made by a king thousands of miles away. This decree strengthened the growing tension between the crown and the colonists and did little to stop the settlements of western lands.

DANIEL BOONE

Daniel Boone was a restless man who found more enjoyment in hunting with his faithful gun, Tick Licker, and traipsing through the woods than he did in farming. When he went on his first hunting trip to Kentucky, he and the men with him stayed for two years. These forages became known as long hunts, and those who participated in them were known as long hunters.

After returning from his trip, Boone made plans to bring his family to Kentucky. Sadly, his initial attempt to settle the land was abandoned when Indians attacked the traveling settlers and killed Boone's son, James, along with several other men. Planting a settlement in Kentucky seemed out of the question until Boone's wealthy friend Judge Richard Henderson proposed buying the land from the Cherokee Indians. Although several of the chiefs agreed to sell the land, one farseeing chief named Dragging Canoe warned that the white men would eventually push them off their land if they gave them a foothold. Dragging Canoe also gave a warning to those who intended on settling in Kentucky, saying it would be a "dark and bloody ground."

Henderson hired Boone to build a road to the newly acquired land, which was aptly dubbed "the Wilderness Road." While Henderson planned his new colony, Transylvania, Boone and a group of men cut a trail through three hundred miles of forest and brush. In some places the road was so narrow that not even a wagon could get through. Once the men crossed the Cumberland Gap, they descended from the mountains into Kentucky.

With the completion of the Wilderness Road in 1775, pioneers began pouring into the area despite the constant Indian attacks. Boone brought his family to Kentucky via the Wilderness Road and established a settlement named Boonesborough. His wife, Rebecca, and daughter, Jemima, were said to be the first white women to stand on the bank of the Kentucky River.

Unfortunately, the settlers had little time to enjoy the scenery, because when the Revolutionary War began, the British encouraged their Indian allies to attack the loosely scattered settlements on the frontier. So much violence took place that 1777 was gruelingly remembered as "the Year of the Bloody Sevens."

All along the frontier, the pioneers suffered from the raids initiated by the British, until a bold man named George Rogers Clark put a daring plan into action. George Rogers Clark was a major in the Virginia militia and the elder brother of William Clark, who would become famous years later in the Lewis and Clark Expedition. With only a handful of men, somewhere between 130 and 170, Clark ventured deep into the British-held Northwest Territory. He attacked and captured several British forts, including Kaskaskia and Vincennes. Using his influence, he negotiated with several of the Indian tribes to stop marauding the frontier.

Clark's actions renewed Virginia's claims to the Northwest Territory and earned him the title "Conqueror of the Northwest." Although the Indians still fought against the settlers, Clark's valiant measures slowed them down and gave the people on the frontier hope for peace.

The Northwest Territory was a large area that included the current states of Ohio, Indiana, Illinois, Michigan, and Wisconsin. This territory was claimed by many of the original colonies, including Virginia, Massachusetts, Connecticut, and New York. After the American Revolution, these states gave their claims to Congress. To help pay the debts of the new nation, Congress sold five million acres in 1787. That same year, they passed the Northwest Ordinances, which stated that only three to five states could be formed from the lands of the Northwest Territory and that slavery must forever be banned from these new states.

Cleverly, Congress laid the foundation in the Northwest Ordinance for admitting new states. When a territory had reached a population of sixty thousand, it could apply for statehood, and new states would receive a status equal to the original thirteen.

Perhaps the best picture of the United States' westward expansion can be seen in the new states that were added to the Union. In 1791, Vermont was added as the fourteenth state, followed by Kentucky in 1792, Tennessee in 1796, and Ohio in 1803. Many of the settlers in the west were veterans from the Revolutionary War who were given land as payment for their services.

To the south of the Northwest Territory and Kentucky was the land of Tennessee, where in 1770, James Robertson escorted a group of settlers. Although Robertson had visited Kentucky with Boone, he preferred the territory claimed by North Carolina, which is now known as Tennessee. After the American Revolution, Congress asked the states to give up their holdings in the west. The people of Tennessee resented being transferred without their consent and formed their own state, calling it Franklin. Briskly, the differences were worked out, and Tennessee soon became part of the Union.

There were numerous reasons that people moved west. Many of the eastern farmers had exhausted the soil because they did not rotate their fields. Large families had only one farm to leave as an inheritance, and it went to the eldest son, leaving the younger sons to seek land out west where the soil was fertile and prices were inexpensive. Glowing letters were sent from friends and family who had moved west, praising the land and abundant game. Some folks just wanted more elbow room, and others were searching for a better life.

These ordinary people who carved a home out of the wilderness helped form the United States of America as it is today. With the same spirit of the people who first settled the new world, they continued to push west.

Digging Deeper

What was the Proclamation of 1763? Did it stop people from settling in the west?

What road did Daniel Boone build?

Who was called the Conqueror of the Northwest?

Who helped settle Tennessee?

Find and read a biography about one of the frontiersmen in this chapter, such as Daniel Boone, George Rogers Clark, or James Robertson.

On a modern atlas, find the various states that were mentioned in this chapter. In a notebook, write down the states in this chapter that you have visited, and record your own observations of the geography, culture, etc. of these states.

Look up early westward expansion in an encyclopedia or read about the settlements of Kentucky, Ohio, and Tennessee.

Pretend that you are a settler on the frontier and are captured by the Indians during one of their raids. You find a bit of paper and decide to keep a journal of what happened. Use your imagination and have fun with this one.

Chapter 11

To the Shores of Tripoli
The Barbary Coast Wars

Along the northern coast of Africa were four countries—Morocco, Algeria, Tunis, and Tripoli (Libya)—that made up what was known as the Barbary Coast. These Muslim nations harbored and sent out notorious pirates who raided coastal towns and attacked merchant ships. Terror was their most dangerous weapon. Preying on weak enemies, they made slaves of those they captured.

For centuries, the nations of Europe purchased a weak, never-lasting peace by paying tribute to the Barbary Coast. Regrettably, the pirates never honored their treaties and continued their appalling acts. This was the established custom of handling affairs in the Mediterranean when the United States gained her independence.

Since America was no longer protected by England, the Barbary countries began to attack ships from the United States. In 1796, America negotiated a treaty with Algeria that promised the initial amount of $642,500 and an annual tribute of naval stores equaling $21,600. This treaty released American sailors being held as slaves. Similar treaties were signed with Tunis, Morocco, and Tripoli. Scarcely was the treaty signed, however, when the four

Barbary countries began complaining that their neighbors had received better gifts than they did. Relations became so strained that on May 14, 1801, the Bashaw of Tripoli declared war against the United States.

Grimly, America entered another war, knowing they must protect their citizens and commerce. In 1798, the United States created the Navy Department. After Thomas Jefferson was elected president, he named Richard Dale as commodore.

News of Tripoli's declaration of war had not reached America when Dale's squadron departed for the Mediterranean. They were merely a "squadron of observation." Once the fleet reached the Mediterranean, however, Dale learned that America was at war. Passing through Gibraltar, he sailed for Tripoli, the capital city of Tripoli, to set up a blockage of the harbor. During Dale's command, the American ship *Enterprise* defeated the *Tripoli*. This victory gave the U.S. sailors the confidence they needed to face the Tripoli pirates, whom everyone thought invincible. In 1802, Dale resigned when another man was promoted to the rank above him.

The navy's second commodore was Captain Richard Valentine Morris. Lacking leadership ability, Morris unfortunately accomplished very little during his command. Bringing along his wife and young son, he gave the impression of going on a pleasure cruise instead of visiting a war zone. Lazily, Morris and his fleet sailed in the Mediterranean.

In February 1803, Morris visited the America consul at Tunis, where he showed his incompetence by allowing himself to be captured and held for ransom. When the Bey of Tunis received $22,000, he released the commodore. Although his fleet had been in the Mediterranean for over a year, Morris did not reach the harbor of Tripoli until May 1803. Displeased with Morris's actions, the United States recalled and court-martialed him.

Edward Preble, the navy's next commodore, was a brave, fearless man who embodied the American spirit of patriotism and ingenuity. When he took command, he began executing plans decisively and with firmness. Immediately upon reaching the Mediterranean, he began negotiating with Morocco, which was threatening to proclaim war against America. His tactics were intimidation instead of tribute. Morocco agreed to peace. Next, Preble tightened the blockade at Tripoli.

An unfortunate event happened on October 31, 1803, when the *Philadelphia* struck a reef near Tripoli. The Tripolitans sailed out to her, where they happily accepted the surrender of the *Philadelphia's* captain, William Bainbridge. The loss of the *Philadelphia* was heightened when the Tripolitans freed the ship from the reef and began preparations to use it against America. If the Tripolitans repaired the *Philadelphia,* it could be a formidable enemy used against the United States. The ship had to be destroyed!

Lieutenant Stephen Decatur volunteered to lead the expedition. The plan was to sail the *Intrepid*, a Tripolitan-style ship that had just been captured, into the harbor, moor her alongside the *Philadelphia*, clear the decks of the enemy, fill the ship with combustibles, and blow her to pieces.

On a dark February night in 1804, the *Intrepid* sailed unnoticed into the Tripoli harbor. Stealing close to the *Philadelphia,* the *Intrepid* sailed directly under the castle guns. At ten o'clock the Tripolitan officer on the *Philadelphia* haled the *Intrepid*. He was kept talking as the two ships drifted closer together. Quickly, the Americans boarded the *Philadelphia* and won the deck. The combustibles were set in place and the fuse lit before the city of Tripoli knew what was happening.

The *Philadelphia* had drifted close to the castle when she exploded. In less than half an hour the Americans had accomplished their mission. Only one sailor was wounded. The *Philadelphia's* destruction prevented her from being used against her own people.

Preble began attacking Tripoli in earnest, but sadly Congress replaced Preble with Captain Samuel Barron. While waiting for the new commodore, Preble made every attempt to finish the war. He decided to send a fire ship into the harbor to destroy the galleys and castle. Lieutenant Richard Somers volunteered to command the enterprise.

After the *Intrepid* was chosen to be the fire ship, she was loaded with one hundred barrels of gunpowder, one hundred and fifty charged shells, and a handful of volunteers. On the night of September 4, 1804, the *Intrepid* sailed into the harbor. Originally the plan was to set the fuse and then abandon the ship with the timing set so that it would blow up at the most advantageous spot. But something went terribly wrong when suddenly the *Intrepid* exploded before reaching its destination. It was thought that Tripolitan ships intercepted the *Intrepid*.

Preble explained, "The gallant Somers and heroes of his party, observing the other three boats surrounding them, and no prospect of escape, determined, at once, to prefer death and the destruction of the enemy to captivity and torturing slavery, put a match to the train leading directly to the magazine, which at once blew the whole into the air, and terminated their existence." Unfortunately the fire ship did not accomplish its mission. All the men on board perished. However, before Barron arrived, Preble made five successful attacks against Tripoli.

Captain Samuel Barron lacked initiative and also suffered greatly from a liver problem. American Consul William Eaton accomplished the only thing of note during Barron's command. Eaton tried to regain the throne of Tripoli for the rightful heir.

Bashaw Yusuf of Tripoli was a greedy, arrogant man. Although Yusuf (Joseph) was the youngest of three sons, he became Bashaw by brutally murdering his eldest brother, Hassan. When Hamet, the middle brother, discovered he was to share his older brother's fate, he escaped to Tunis, where he met Eaton and later fled to Egypt.

After Tripoli opened hostilities against the United States, the idea of helping Hamet reclaim the throne as a means of regaining peace seemed like a good strategy. In 1804, Eaton was sent to Egypt to find Hamet and offer to help him overthrow his brother. After Eaton found the banished brother, a small force was gathered, consisting of Hamet's followers, a small number of Greeks, seven marines, and one lieutenant. On March 6, 1805, they began a strenuous march across the Libyan Desert.

Traveling throughout the vast wasteland, they suffered from lack of food and water, and mutiny among Hamet's followers. Finally, on April 24, they reached the outskirts of the Tripoli town of Derna. Several days later, they, along with three American ships, captured the city. Hamet could taste victory. Eaton knew a lasting peace would be established between the two countries after Hamet was on the throne.

Sadly for both men, the United States and Tripoli had already begun peace talks before the battle at Derna. Bashaw Yusuf feared his brother would obtain the throne and thought it wise to begin peace negotiations. Since Barron would not fight, and the Consul General for Barbary, Tobias Lear, disliked the Hamet expedition, the peace treaty was completed on June 10, 1805. The agreement released the *Philadelphia* crew and gave America freedom to trade in the Mediterranean unmolested.

The Barbary Coast was peaceful for a time, but soon they began their age-old trade of piracy again. Finally, after the War of 1812, President Madison sent a fleet to Algeria to settle the matter. Stephen Decatur subdued the tyrants, and never again were the Americans threatened by terrorizing pirates in the Mediterranean.

Digging Deeper

What four countries made up the Barbary States? Find them on a globe or map of the world.

Between what countries was the Barbary War fought?

Make a list of important characters in the Barbary War and their accomplishments.

In many ways the Barbary War was considered America's first war against terror. *Jefferson's War* by Joseph Wheelan does an excellent job of covering the war.

After reading the book mentioned above, make a time line of events that happened during the Barbary War, or make a time line from the events mentioned in this chapter.

What impact did the Barbary War have on the development of the United States as a nation?

Chapter 12

The Lewis & Clark Expedition

On June 20, 1803, President Thomas Jefferson took out a piece of paper, and dabbing his quill pen in ink, he began to compose a letter of instruction to his personal secretary and friend, Meriwether Lewis. Part of the letter said, "The object of your mission is to explore the Missouri river, & such principal stream of it, as, by its course & communication with the water of the Pacific Ocean may offer the most direct & practicable water communication across this continent, for the purposes of commerce."

Thomas Jefferson had long dreamed of sending an expedition to improve knowledge of the unknown west. When the United States purchased the Louisiana Territory from France for fifteen million dollars in April 1803, his hopes were about to come true. The additional land more than doubled the size of the nation. America now owned the land that Jefferson had been longing to have explored.

Jefferson could not have found a more able, active, and adventurous man to lead the group than Meriwether Lewis. Born in 1774 near Charlottesville, Virginia, Meriwether was the eldest son of William and Lucy Lewis. When he was thirteen, his formal education began, some of which he learned under Benjamin Rush, a signer of the Declaration of Independence. Excitedly, Lewis joined the militia when the Whiskey Rebellion broke out in 1794. Lewis later enlisted in the army and was assigned to the Chosen Rifle Company, where William Clark served as captain. A strong friendship soon formed between Lewis and Clark. When Lewis was asked to lead the expedition, he instantly requested his friend, William Clark, to accompany him as co-commander.

William Clark was also born in Virginia, but he moved with his family to Kentucky at the age of fourteen. On the unsettled frontier, he learned valuable skills about survival in the wild. Although Clark had no formal education, he was able to read and write. In 1789, at the age of nineteen, William joined the Kentucky Militia and later went into the army, where he was promoted to the rank of captain. Clark and Lewis both shared a love for the outdoors and adventure. William Clark was a determined, diligent and daring man, a wonderful combination on a dangerous journey.

WILLIAM CLARK & MERIWETHER LEWIS

Lewis, Clark, and the Corps of Discovery—a group of tough men who were willing to face the trials of the journey—embarked from St. Louis in May, 1804. Traveling in a keelboat through the present-day states of Missouri, Kansas, Nebraska, Iowa, and South and North Dakota, they sailed up the Missouri River.

As winter began to settle in, the group built Fort Mandan, where they spent the winter. The river had become congested with ice, and the explorers had to wait for spring before they could continue. Wisely, Lewis and Clark demonstrated their desire to become friends with the Mandan Indians whom the fort was named after. When the chief of the Mandan Indians was presented with a peace medal that had a silhouette of Jefferson on one side and a picture of two hands clasping with the words "Peace and Friendship" adorning the other side, he was very pleased with Lewis and Clark. The first leg of their journey had been successful!

During the winter, Lewis and Clark hired a French-Canadian fur trapper named Toussaint Charbonneau and his Shoshoni wife, Sacagawea, to act as interpreters. On February 11, 1805, Sacagawea gave birth to a son, Jean Baptiste Charbonneau, whom Clark later nicknamed Pomp.

When Sacagawea was a little girl, she had been captured by the Hidatsa Indians and later sold to Charbonneau. The presence of a woman and child with the Corps would show the Indians that they were not a war party. Sacagawea proved to be a capable guide and excellent interpreter, and she was very calm and collected in emergencies.

On April 7, 1805, they bade farewell to Fort Mandan and headed west. When the party reached a fork in the Missouri, Lewis and Clark conferred together to determine which of the forks to take. Most of the men were of the opinion that the North Fork was the Missouri, but Lewis and Clark mutually agreed that the South Fork would lead them to the mouth of the river, so that route was the one taken.

The upper regions of the Missouri were heavily infested with ferocious grizzly bears that proved quite troublesome to the Corps. Lewis thanked God for divine protection against the deadly creatures.

The Indians had informed them about the Great Falls, in modern-day Montana, but nothing could have prepared them for the magnificent series of waterfalls they encountered. Presenting a huge obstacle to the explorers, the falls took them nearly a month to portage around.

As they continued along the Missouri, the river became narrower and more difficult to navigate. The party desperately needed to find the Shoshoni Indians to purchase horses so they could travel overland.

Fatigued and weary, the group pressed on, cheered by the courageous examples of Clark and Lewis. They passed the Continental Divide at Lemhi Pass. Finally, they found the Shoshoni Indians encamped beside the cool, clear waters of Lemhi River. The Indians provided horses. On October 16, 1805, the Corps reached the Columbia River, where the friendly Yakima Indians greeted them. They journeyed down the Columbia River, passing the magnificent Celilo Falls and The Dalles.

The long-awaited Pacific Ocean was finally reached in November, 1805. Along the beautiful seashore, the group found a whale that had been washed up on shore. Purchasing as much of the blubber and oil as the Indians would sell them, the Corps was delighted at the unexpected treat. Clark remarked that he was glad God had sent the whale for them to consume, instead of, like Jonah, to devour them! Building another winter camp, they named it Fort Clatsop in honor of the natives.

Their homeward journey began on March 23, 1806. Before departing from Fort Clatsop, Lewis and Clark had decided to split up the group at Travelers Rest so they could explore more territory and better improve their understanding of the lay of the land. Their rendezvous was the place where the Yellowstone River meets the Missouri.

While it took them nearly a year and a half to reach the Pacific, the return trip only took them seven months. They reached St. Louis on September 23, 1806. Since they had been gone for over two years, most people assumed they had perished on the journey. Great celebrations were held in St. Louis on their return. They had made it home at last!

The Lewis and Clark Expedition threw wide the doors for western expansion. Unlocking the trails of the unknown west, Lewis and Clark prepared the way to be followed by mountain men, adventure-seekers, and later, hardworking settlers. Their journey gave the world a new, rugged land that became a beacon to courageous people who were seeking new life in an untamed territory.

Lewis, Clark, and the men with them were the first recorded white men to cross the North American continent. Wind, rain, and time may have washed away the footprints they made on the land, but the mark they made on history has been preserved. Their heroism, courage, and trials will be remembered. They were willing to brave the unknown, never looking back to what was left behind, but pushing onward to their destination. May God find us with the same zeal pressing toward the goals He has given us.

Digging Deeper

Look on a map to see the size of the Louisiana Purchase. How many present-day states were a part of the Louisiana Territory?

When did Lewis and Clark leave St. Louis? When did they return?

Name Sacagawea's native tribe.

Study the different tribes of Native Americans. Some of the Indians that Lewis and Clark met were the Shoshoni, Sioux, Blackfeet, Nez Perce, and Flatheads. How did they make a living? What did they use for food and clothing? How did they use the natural resources that surrounded them?

Try drawing a map. It can even be a map of your own backyard or neighborhood. Just have fun with it!

Play *The Lewis and Clark Adventure Game* by Educational Insights, a thrilling board game that is good for third grade and up.

Lewis and Clark for Kids by Janis Herbert has twenty-one fun activities for hands-on learning. (Caution: some of the material in this book is evolutionary, but it is still a good resource.)

Cooking on the Lewis and Clark Expedition by Mary Gunderson is a great book with simple recipes of foods eaten on the trip.

Chapter 13

Miracle at New Orleans

The American victory at the Battle of New Orleans during the War of 1812 was an amazing miracle! When looking at the facts, there was no possible reason for the American success except the hand of God working on their behalf.

The battle was actually fought after the war was over. The peace treaty had been signed on December 24, 1814, in Ghent, Netherlands, but the Battle of New Orleans took place on January 8, 1815. At this time in history, the world lacked the means to communicate important information quickly, and neither the American nor the British armies in the New Orleans area knew the war was over.

If the British had arrived in New Orleans when they had planned, it would have been an easy triumph for them, but there was a Providential delay. God also provided an unusual ally for the Americans: Jean Lafitte, a notorious pirate. Completely outnumbered, the Americans under General Jackson should have been beaten, but God, who controls everything, fought for the Americans and they won.

God graciously allowed the mistakes of one man to delay the entire British fleet that was gathering at Jamaica with the intent of sailing for New Orleans. Three British man-of-war ships under the command of Captain Lloyd saw an American privateer, the *General Armstrong*, anchored at a port in the Azores Islands. According to the rules of war, the English could not attack the American ship since it was docked in a neutral port, but the zealous captain attacked the ship anyway. A desperate fight began. The Americans fought valiantly! Vastly outnumbered, the Americans sank their own ship and fled to land. The victory had been costly for the British, with three hundred casualties. Meanwhile, the British fleet at Jamaica had postponed their intended departure for ten days, waiting for Captain Lloyd. This delay allowed the Americans time to prepare for the battle. God was in control!

America found a friend in one of the most unlikely places: in the pirate Jean Lafitte. Jean Lafitte and his brother, Pierre, had arrived in New Orleans a few years before in 1809, and they began a blacksmith shop that was really a cover-up for their profitable business of selling contraband goods. Although Jean said he and the one thousand fighting men under his command were privateers, they were in truth pirates. The base of his operation was an island named Barataria, which was called the "back door to New Orleans" because the island controlled the bayous and swamps between New Orleans and the Gulf.

For many years the clever, creative, cunning Jean Lafitte was very successful. The American government had tried to rid New Orleans of the outlaw, but all of their efforts failed. Before the Battle of New Orleans, Governor Claiborne offered five hundred dollars for the capture of Jean Lafitte. The next day, Claiborne's wanted poster was gone and another hung in its place, offering fifteen hundred dollars for the capture of Governor Claiborne and signed by Jean Lafitte. The pirate had a sense of humor!

Seeing the strategic position of Barataria, the British attempted to obtain the pirate's aid in capturing New Orleans. They offered him a commission in the Royal Navy, land, and thirty thousand pounds, but to their request and gift he gave evasive answers, saying he needed time to think about it. Strangely, Jean then took the letters he had received from the English to New Orleans, warned them of the British attack, and offered his services. Lafitte also provided musket flints and powder, which the Americans desperately needed. During the Battle of New Orleans, Lafitte and his men fought courageously. Later they were given a pardon by President Madison, but not long afterward Jean returned to his piracy.

What made Lafitte side with the Americans? As a pirate he had no loyalty except to himself. If Lafitte had helped the English, it is possible the Battle of New Orleans would have turned out differently. God can use anyone, even a godless pirate!

BATTLE OF NEW ORLEANS

Leading the Americans who stood between the British and New Orleans was the bold Andrew Jackson from Tennessee. He was born on March 15, 1767. Even though he was just a boy, he fought in the American Revolution. During that war, he was captured by the British and ordered to clean an officer's boots, but the young Jackson passionately refused. The officer slashed Andrew on the cheek with his sword, leaving a prominent scar. Jackson was always proud of how he got that scar. Many years later, when the War of 1812 broke out, Jackson, who was in his forties, raised troops to help conquer the ambitious British.

Andrew Jackson was a determined man, a courteous gentleman, and a fierce general; he was nicknamed Old Hickory by his men because he was as hard as hickory wood. There could not have been an abler man sent to defend the city of New Orleans. God brought the right man along at America's darkest hour.

During the closing days of December, 1814, several small skirmishes took place between the two enemies. On January 8, 1815, the greatest battle began—the Battle of New Orleans. The Americans were outnumbered more than two to one. The British had twelve thousand soldiers while America had around five thousand men.

Industriously, the Americans constructed a crude entrenchment of earth and logs along the Rodriguez Canal, which was a dry ditch. The British troops, under General Pakenham, the brother-in-law of Wellington, were overconfident of their ability. After all, they had just defeated Napoleon, the greatest military genius the world had ever seen, and here they were fighting backwoodsmen and farmers!

God humbles the plans of the proud! When the English advanced, the Americans began a devastating fire of musketry. General Jackson's army was made up of men from Kentucky, Tennessee, volunteers from New Orleans, and the pirates from Barataria. The men from Kentucky were known as excellent marksmen and sharpshooters.

Despite the heavy fire, the English kept advancing. Keeping up a determined discharge of bullets, the Americans went about their bloody work. At last the fatal blow came to the British when General Pakenham was shot down while trying to rally his men. The English retreated.

It had been a hard and grueling day for the Americans, but a devastating day for the British. Suffering few losses, the Americans had eight men killed and thirteen wounded while the English had over two thousand killed or wounded, including many officers. The British were defeated. The fighting ended. America won! God brought about a great victory!

Although the battle had no effect on the outcome of the war, it was definitely not a useless encounter. The victory at the Battle of New Orleans gained America the respect of other countries and gave the United States a strong sense of national pride. Up to that point, individuals still saw themselves as citizens of their respective states, but with the conclusion of the war, the people professed a firm dedication to the union and found delight in being Americans. They truly became the United States of America.

Sadly, the people did not give God the glory for their triumph as the Founding Fathers had done. Andrew Jackson was one of the few who saw that it was God who had brought about the victories. God is still God whether we acknowledge His power or deny it. May we be a people who see the miracles God has performed through the pages of history and give Him the glory due His name!

Digging Deeper

What caused the War of 1812? How long did the war last? Who was president at the time of the war?

On a map, find New Orleans, Barataria, and Jamaica.

What is the difference between a pirate and a privateer?

Read a biography about Andrew Jackson.

Although the War of 1812 is not a very well-known war, it is very interesting to study. A good resource that recounts the war is *From Sea to Shining Sea* by Peter Marshall and David Manuel. Read the chapters "Don't Give Up the Ship" and "The Dawn's Early Light."

Some topics for study: The British practice of impressing American sailors, the burning of Washington, Francis Scott Key and the writing of the Star-Spangled Banner, and the history of Louisiana. (Consider that it had only been a part of the United States since the Louisiana Purchase). An encyclopedia would be a good resource to learn about these topics.

Pretend you are a soldier with Andrew Jackson in New Orleans. Write a letter home telling about the battle.

Chapter 14

The Second Great Awakening

After winning their War for Independence against the most powerful nation in the world, the people of America became confident in their own abilities. They no longer relied on God for their very existence. As a result, complacency toward religion and the things of God followed. In the expanding west, a self-reliant attitude reigned, while in the east the people embraced a love of reason.

God wasn't finished with the young nation and its citizens, and in His infinite wisdom He ignited a revival—the Second Great Awakening. Although the methods of revival were different in the east and west, the same Spirit of God changed the infant United States.

The first spark of the Second Great Awakening occurred in one of the most unlikely places—a wild and reckless county in Kentucky. Logan County earned the nickname "Rogues' Harbor" because of the outlaws, ruffians, and scoundrels who lived there. Several moral citizens lived there also and were called the "Regulators." When they tried to reform the unruly county, a battle between the "good guys" and "bad guys" followed. But unlike a typical western movie, the good guys were soundly defeated. With the victory of the "Rogues," Logan County became even more lawless.

To this ungodly place came the able Reverend James McGready, a Scotch-Irish Presbyterian, who began shepherding three congregations in the area. During the closing years of the 1700s, McGready's churches began fervently praying for revival. Finally, an awakening of the Spirit took place in July 1799, at the Red River meeting. The following summer, in June of 1800, more than five hundred people gathered for the quarterly communion service held at the Red River in Logan County. Such an outpouring of the Spirit took place that people instantly committed their lives to Christ. What seemed like disorder followed, with some people singing hymns, others falling to their knees with a scream, while still others fell over as though dead. The truth was that conversion took place, and those who had been changed praised God.

Spreading the revival, McGready shared the truth with his other congregations, and they were soon basking in the new freedom of Christ. At the Gasper River camp meeting, an astounding ten thousand people arrived. Some came with open hearts, others with curiosity, and still others to stir up trouble. But as they listened to the message, and through the Spirit's conviction, many gave their lives to Christ. Quickly the waves of revival changed the rough people of Logan County.

One of the largest revival meetings took place in Cane Ridge, Kentucky, in 1801. Barton Stone coordinated the event and invited Presbyterian, Baptist, and Methodist preachers to join him in presenting the gospel on the seven platforms that had been constructed for the meeting. Around twenty-five thousand people attended! Once more revival spread, and soon the awakening swept across the United States.

Keeping the Second Great Awakening alive became the job of circuit riders who carried the message to the far reaches of the country. The most influential circuit rider was a Methodist preacher named Francis Asbury. He divided land into sections, or circuits, and assigned preachers to each circuit.

Arriving in America before the Revolutionary War, Asbury opted to remain in the colonies when John Wesley recalled Methodist ministers because of the impending war. Since the Methodist movement was the first denomination to send preachers to evangelize the frontier, much of that region became associated with that church. Asbury took his calling to reach the lost and encourage the faithful seriously. For years, journeying an average of 6,000 miles annually, Asbury preached at inns, jails, and churches. Through his example of love and self-sacrifice, he inspired other preachers to follow in his footsteps. Powerfully he proclaimed biblical truth, and during his life he personally ordained 4,000 preachers, traveled 300,000 miles, and preached 16,500 sermons! When he died on March 31, 1816, the entire Methodist movement mourned the loss of such a Godly man.

Peter Cartwright, another prominent circuit rider, grew up in the wild "Rogues' Harbor" in Kentucky. At a camp meeting led by James McGready, the rebellious Cartwright gave his life to Jesus, and he became a powerful soldier of Christ. Serving as a Methodist preacher, Cartwright used his booming voice to proclaim the message of Christ to all who would listen. Because of his rough upbringing and personal strength, the rugged people of the frontier respected him and were more willing to listen to him than to other preachers. By his influence ten thousand people accepted Christ, and twenty thousand joined the church.

In the settled east, the people's self-reliance had turned into the worship of the goddess Reason. Deism (which denied the deity of Christ, the inspiration of the Bible, and the reality of miracles) became the most fashionable religion. Fascination with the French Revolution made many embrace the philosophies of that bloody conflict.

In 1794, *The Age of Reason* by Thomas Paine was heartily welcomed. Ushering in the New Age of Rationalism, the deist found a fertile field in the once-Christian east. Before publishing his book, Paine sent a copy to his friend, Benjamin Franklin, to get his thoughts on the work. Franklin replied in a letter, "[T]he consequence of printing this piece will be a great deal of odium [hate] drawn upon yourself, mischief to you, and no benefit to others. He that spits into the wind, spits in his own face. But were you to succeed, do you imagine any good would be done by it? . . . If men are so wicked with religion, what would they be if without it?"

Sadly, Paine rejected Franklin's advice, and a great deal of harm was done because of his book. Many colleges that had been founded on biblical principles embraced these new teachings. The young college students seemed especially susceptible. Jacobin societies that imitated the deistic societies of France sprang up on most college campuses.

Then Timothy Dwight entered the scene, sparked a revival, and halted the French Rationalist ideas. Dwight was the grandson of Jonathan Edwards, the great theologian of the First Great Awakening. In 1795, he became the president of Yale and instantly began reinstating Christian values. He removed the faculty that taught French philosophies, made attending chapel a requirement, and began holding frank discussions with the students. Listening to their arguments, Dwight created an environment where he could share the truths about Christianity and the falsity of the Rationalist.

Although the students respected him, change did not come quickly. At last, through Dwight's diligence and prayers, an awakening broke out in 1802. Nearly half of the college was converted. The French-philosophy-minded students returned to the truths found in the scriptures. By the faithfulness of Timothy Dwight and the power of God, Yale was completely transformed. Revival had spread to the east.

Although the flames of revival had not entirely died out, they were fanned again in the 1820s. God used Charles Finney this time to keep the fire burning. After his conversion in 1821, he began preaching in New York. Revival followed. Instituting "New Measures" in evangelism, Finney blocked off an area called "anxious seats" available for those under conviction. He combined the fiery preaching style of the west with the emotional restraint of the east. His most famous revival took place in Rochester, New York, in 1831, where one tenth of the population became Christians. The entire city changed, and people had a renewed interest in the things of God. As Finney himself said, "Regeneration implies an entire present change of moral character, this is, a change from entire sinfulness to entire holiness." Charles Finney had a vast influence, with an estimated five hundred thousand conversions.

The Second Great Awakening helped unify the newly formed United States. Once again, the church began caring for orphans, widows, and the sick. Many benevolent organizations sprang up, and the birth of the first foreign mission board, the American Board of Commissioners for Foreign Missions, resulted from the Second Great Awakening. The revival gave the United States a stability and strength it had never known before. America became a great nation because she honored the one true God above all others and willingly turned back to God when convicted of her sins. As Alexis de Tocqueville observed in 1831, "America is great because she is good. If American ceases to be good, America will cease to be great."

Digging Deeper

Who were the leading preachers of the Second Great Awakening?

Where was the first spark of revival?

List the major revival meetings mentioned in this chapter.

Read *From Sea to Shining Sea* by Peter Marshall and David Manuel. The events of the Second Great Awakening are covered in the chapters "Like a Mighty River," "On the Stretch for God," "Needles of Light," and "New Wine, New Wineskins."

Visit http://www.revival-library.org. This Web site has many Second Great Awakening documents and quotes.

Use the resources mentioned above to research the Second Great Awakening and then write a paper about the events that you found most interesting.

Chapter 15

Daniel Webster
Defender of the Constitution

During the first half of the 1800s, a brave, bold, benevolent man by the name of Daniel Webster became a leading politician in American government. He spoke eloquently and had the ability to persuade others to his point of view. Because of his work to uphold the Constitution, he became known as the "Defender of the Constitution." Being a devoted Christian, he also knew that government and Christianity must go hand in hand. He once said, "Whatever makes men good Christians, makes them good citizens." The great statesman, Daniel Webster, was both an excellent Christian and a remarkable citizen.

The childhood of the great statesman prepared him for his future career. On January 18, 1782, a sickly child was born to Mr. and Mrs. Ebenezer Webster in Salisbury, New Hampshire. Although Daniel was a delicate child, he had an active mind and learned to read by the age of five. Once, Daniel's schoolteacher offered a jack-knife as a prize to the student who could memorize the most Bible passages. On the day of the contest, Daniel overwhelmed the teacher by reciting one hundred and twenty verses. He would have continued, but the teacher stopped him, declaring Daniel to be the winner.

Young Daniel also loved his country. Using his own money, he purchased a handkerchief with the Constitution of the United States printed on it. He read the words over and over again until they were forever written on his heart. The Bible and the Constitution were the guiding forces throughout his life.

Getting an education proved difficult for the future leader because of his family's financial situation. Clearly, his parents saw his capacity for learning, but they struggled to make ends meet. They made many sacrifices for Daniel to attend Phillips Academy in Exeter, but he became so shy that he was unable to recite his lessons. He returned home after one year.

Over the next few years, Daniel overcame his timidity, studied fervently, and later attended Dartmouth College. During these formative years his speaking abilities blossomed. Having graduated from college, Daniel studied in Boston to become a lawyer and passed the bar exam in 1805. After much sacrifice and hard work, he enjoyed the benefit of a good education.

Daniel Webster was a devoted family man. In 1808, he married Grace Fletcher. The daughter of a minister, Grace shared Daniel's love for Jesus Christ and his devotion to the Christian life. After the wedding, Daniel took his bride to a home he had prepared for her in Portsmouth.

At about this time, God allowed a miracle to take place in Daniel's health. After being sickly during his childhood and early adult years, he started to improve, and he joyfully praised the Healer. The Lord blessed them further with five children: Grace, Daniel Fletcher, Julia, Edward, and Charlie. Their home was a happy one, but sadly his wife died in 1828, and at the time of Daniel's death in 1852, only one of his children survived him. During these trying times when he lost his loved ones, Daniel found comfort in

Christ and the hope of heaven. He married Caroline LeRoy in 1829, and they had many pleasant years together.

In 1812, Daniel Webster entered politics. Fervently he opposed the War of 1812. His views matched the opinions of the people of New Hampshire, and they elected him to represent them in the House of Representatives. Once in the house, he bravely opposed the "war hawks," Henry Clay and John C. Calhoun, who were the driving forces behind the declaration of war. His eloquent speaking abilities gave him immediate recognition.

After serving only one term, Daniel returned to his law practice, much to the disappointment of the people of New Hampshire. In 1816 he moved to Boston. Clearly, the people of Boston saw he was a born leader, and in 1822 he was again elected to the House where he faithfully represented his state.

DANIEL WEBSTER

Becoming president is the ambition of many people who serve in Congress, and Daniel Webster was no exception. In 1835, Daniel Webster was nominated to run for president, but Martin Van Buren won the election. Andrew Jackson said of Daniel, "Mr. Webster won't be nominated because he is too far East, knows too much and is too honest." That statement demonstrated Webster's character.

Although Webster never served as president, he did use his speaking abilities to help others obtain that office, one of whom was William Harrison. Daniel served as Harrison's Secretary of State, and when Harrison died, President John Tyler asked Webster to remain in that position. During his term as Secretary of State, he helped establish a treaty with Great Britain, which determined the boundary between Canada and Maine in a contract called the Webster-Ashburton Treaty.

Although he enjoyed politics, Webster's real delight was debating cases before a court of law. His skills allowed him to argue several important cases before the United States Supreme Court. One of the most interesting cases was *Vidal v. Girard's Executors* in 1844. In his will, Stephen Girard left his property to the city of Philadelphia to be made into an orphanage and college. However, he also stated that no minister or Christian could teach at the institution. Webster argued that a school's success depended on a Christian foundation. He said, "No fault can be found with Girard for wishing a marble college to bear his name for ever, but it is not valuable unless it has a fragrance of Christianity about it." The court ruled in Webster's favor. Effectively, Daniel argued many other cases before the Supreme Court.

Daniel was a silver-tongued orator and spoke at many important historical events. When the bicentennial of the Pilgrims' landing came in 1820, Webster was requested to give an inspiring oration. He also spoke at the commemoration service for Thomas Jefferson and John

Adams. Addressing the people who gathered at the fiftieth anniversary of the Battle of Bunker Hill, Webster praised the men who gave so much for freedom. When he spoke of the United States he loved and to the citizens he loved, his black eyes would shine with emotion.

In 1827, the people of Massachusetts sent the illustrious statesman to the Senate. During his first term, Webster gave his greatest oration in defense of the Constitution. "The Reply to Hayne," as the speech has become known, fervently declared the Constitution as the supreme law of the land that cannot be overruled by the states. He concluded with the words, "Liberty and Union, now and forever, one and inseparable!" His speech influenced America for years to come.

Another remarkable speech Webster gave in the Senate was during the debate over the Compromise of 1850. Although Daniel opposed slavery personally, he saw the ties between North and South weakening, and he knew it would take a compromise to preserve the Union. His "Seventh of May Speech" promoted the Compromise of 1850. His fellow citizens in the North were angry with him for endorsing the Compromise, especially because of the Fugitive Slave Act that it included, but Daniel believed the Union must be saved. He put the needs of the country above his own personal opinions.

Daniel Webster died two years later on October 24, 1852. He was a steadfast Christian and one of the greatest statesmen America has ever seen, rightly called the "Defender of the Constitution" because of the impressive way he promoted the unity of America. May we be like Daniel Webster, who utilized his talents to honor God and serve his country.

Digging Deeper

Where and when was Daniel Webster born? What was his occupation?

On a sheet of paper, list the accomplishments of Daniel Webster.

Memorize this quote by Daniel Webster: "Whatever makes men good Christians, makes them good citizens." Discuss what Webster meant by this statement.

Read *Daniel Webster* by Robert Allen, a good book that gives a general overview of his life.

Look up the following in an encyclopedia: Henry Clay, John C. Calhoun, Webster-Ashburton Treaty, Compromise of 1850, and Fugitive Slave Act.

Read Daniel Webster's "The Bunker Hill Oration" (*The Patriot's Handbook* by George Grant, PH.D. contains the lecture). Imagine you are a journalist for a national newspaper, and write an article about the day's events. Note: the famous Revolutionary War hero Lafayette was also there to lay the cornerstone of the Bunker Hill Monument.

Attend a TeenPact class. This four-day government class for students ages 13–18 is amazing. Visit their Web site at www.teenpact.com to see if there is a class in your state.

Research the legislative process and then have a mock legislative session with your family.

Chapter 16

The Mexican War
America Expands in the Southwest

In the 1840s, the United States found itself embroiled in war with its neighbor to the south, the country of Mexico. Caused by disagreements about the border between Texas and Mexico, this noteworthy dispute became known as the Mexican War. It was this conflict that helped America reach her potential of stretching from sea to shining sea.

During the early 1800s, what is known today as Texas belonged to Mexico, along with most of the rest of the southwestern region of the United States. Only a few Mexicans occupied their northern territory, and they were constantly plagued by attacks from the Comanche Indians.

To help settle the area of Texas, the Mexican government decided to open the region to Americans. Allowed to purchase land for a mere $1.25 per acre, they were required to become Mexican citizens, promise to obey Mexican laws, and embrace the Catholic religion. The settlers felt that what they gained was much more than what they gave—they were free from taxes and levies and were allowed to govern themselves. Initially they suffered from Indian attacks, but the Comanches soon learned to leave the fierce Americans alone.

Stephen Austin brought the first three hundred settlers to Texas in 1821. Nine years later, sixteen thousand people inhabited the region. This influx prompted Mexico to prohibit more settlers from moving into the area, and they sent soldiers to Texas to keep an eye on the Americans. Naturally, there were many Texans who wanted to maintain peace with Mexico. Among them was Stephen Austin, but when he was arrested as part of a peaceful delegation to Mexico City, he began to change his mind. After his release, he returned to Texas to prepare for battle. Mexico sent their president, Antonio Lopez de Santa Anna, to subdue the rebellious north.

As the Mexican troops neared San Antonio, the American populace gathered in the old mission called the Alamo. Santa Anna, who called himself "the Napoleon of the West," planned to surprise the Texans by attacking in the winter. When he arrived on February 23, 1836, the people of San Antonio either quickly left town or found shelter at the Alamo. Colonel Jim Bowie and Colonel William Barrett Travis shared command of the fort until Bowie was suddenly taken ill.

One of Santa Anna's first actions was to hoist a crimson flag high on the bell tower of the San Fernando Church to inform the defenders that no quarter would be given. Travis answered the villainous threat by firing an eighteen-pounder. To further dishearten the Texans, Santa Anna had the song of no mercy, "Deguello," played night and day. Travis's many pleas for help went unheeded except for thirty-two brave men who came from Gonzales on the eighth day of the conflict.

On March 6, 1836, Santa Anna ordered what would be the final attack. Four thousand Mexicans advanced. Cutting down the first row of soldiers, the expert marksmen of the Alamo beat back the onslaught. Three times the defenders repelled Santa Anna's men, and three times they regrouped and attacked again.

With each assault, the numbers in the Alamo decreased until there were not enough to prevent the Mexicans from scaling the walls. Around each Texan lay corpses of Mexicans who had fallen in hand-to-hand conflict. It had been a costly victory for Mexico, with 1,600 dead and another 500 wounded. Unfortunately the 182 defenders of the Alamo had perished.

However, Santa Anna's glory was to be short-lived. He was defeated and captured by Sam Houston on the San Jacinto River. Agreeing to peace, Santa Anna left Texas and acknowledged it as an independent country.

The Republic of Texas wished to join the United States, but President Andrew Jackson concluded that this might lead to war with Mexico. Plus, the hot issue of whether it would be admitted as a free state or a slave state kept Texas out of the Union for nearly ten years. Finally, in March 1845, the United States annexed Texas, and it became the twenty-eighth state.

Disputes soon arose about the border between Mexico and the United States. Mexico recognized the border as the Nueces River, while Texas claimed it was the Rio Grande. A peaceful agreement was attempted when President James K. Polk sent John Slidell to Mexico. The diplomatic attempt did not solve the disagreements, and President Polk sent General Zachary Taylor with troops into the disputed area.

Taylor and his men set up camp on the north side of the Rio Grande while a Mexican force was across the river at Matamoros. In April of 1846, the Mexicans attacked an American patrol, thus beginning the Mexican War. General Taylor, who was called "Old Rough and Ready," and two thousand soldiers met five thousand Mexicans under General Arista at the Battle of Palo Alto in May. Although vastly outnumbered, the Americans won.

Early victories encouraged people back home, and when President Polk called for fifty thousand volunteers, the quota was quickly met. During the summer of 1845, the United States won several battles. They even traveled into Mexico and attacked Monterrey. It took over a month of fatiguing travel though a barren desert to reach the city, and after five days of hard fighting, the outnumbered Americans captured the town. Taylor, who thought this victory would end the war, offered generous terms to the vanquished enemy and agreed to an eight-week truce for peace talks. Unfortunately, however, the war continued.

Back in Washington, Polk grew nervous because Taylor was becoming such a national hero that some were talking about having him run for president. Wishing to push Taylor out of the spotlight, Polk appointed General Winfield Scott to lead the next assault.

Scott, along with nine thousand men from Taylor's army, set sail for Vera Cruz. This left Taylor with only a small force when the treacherous Santa Anna arrived on February 22, 1847. During the ensuing Battle of Buena Vista, the Mexicans attacked quickly and vigorously, hoping to gain a decisive victory. Although drastically outnumbered, the Americans again emerged triumphant. With six thousand Americans against twenty thousand Mexicans, it is a miracle that only about seven hundred and fifty Americans were killed or missing, while Mexico lost half her force. Under the cover of darkness, Santa Anna retreated.

General Scott, with twelve thousand troops, began to attack Vera Cruz in March of 1847. The captain of engineers, Robert E. Lee, served as Scott's right-hand man. Heavy bombardment of the town began on March 23, and soon after Vera Cruz surrendered. Great respect and courtesy was shown to the defeated.

With one victory behind them, Scott led his men on a march to Mexico City. It might seem crazy to us to think of Scott's army of eighty thousand five hundred traveling through hundreds of miles of hostile country, but that's exactly what they did. On a mountain called Cerro Gordo, Santa Anna set up defenses that seemed to him impassable. Robert E. Lee found a way though the chaparral and underbrush on the left flank and surprised the Mexicans, who thought themselves secure. Before the battle was lost, Santa Anna abandoned his men and fled. Generously, Scott paroled the three thousand prisoners and continued toward Mexico City.

Much time was lost while Scott awaited reinforcements. Eventually, he called up all the men who were garrisoning towns. This brought his army to over ten thousand men. Before them lay Mexico City.

That magnificent town, with its lakes and raised causeways, seemed impossible to capture. A costly battle was fought at a bridge over the Churubusco River. On August 22, 1847, a two-week armistice began. However, it was not peace that the Mexicans wanted, but more time. When Scott realized this, his army advanced.

At the capture of Chapultepec Castle, Captain Thomas Jackson showed uncommon bravery when he almost single-handedly took out a Mexican gun battery. Lieutenant U.S. Grant also showed rare valor at the Belen Gate when he placed a gun in the belfry of a church and bombarded the Mexicans. Finally, the Americans captured the city and raised the Stars and Stripes over the National Palace— called the Halls of Montezuma—on September 14, 1847.

The Treaty of Guadalupe Hidalgo was signed on February 2, 1848, thus ending the Mexican War. Mexico acknowledged the Rio Grande as their border and turned over most of what is the American southwest to the United States.

The Mexican War was fought at the same time that the question of slavery and the growing tension between the North and South was plaguing the United States. Because of this, the Mexican War can easily be overlooked in history. However, this conflict had a considerable influence on the United States, greatly expanding its territory in the west. In addition, Zachary Taylor, having gained a considerable national reputation during the Mexican War, would later go on to become president, and many of the men who fought in the Civil War received their first taste of battle in the conflict with Mexico.

Digging Deeper

When did the Mexican War begin? When did it end?

Name some of the men who died at the Alamo.

Who were some of the Civil War heroes who fought in the Mexican War?

Would the Mexican War be better known if the Civil War had not taken place?

Find the places mentioned in this chapter on a map.

Read about the Mexican War in an encyclopedia.

Chapter 17

The Oregon Trail
Road to the American Promised Land

Since the early days of America's history, brave pioneers had been instrumental in opening up new land and claiming it from the wilderness. This same spirit of adventure had been steadily moving people west since the days of the Pilgrims, but by the mid-1800s, the farmers had reached the western plains, which they thought were not suitable for agriculture. These people heard that across the prairie and over the rugged mountains was a land that was fertile. Some stories told about Oregon were true, but others were so exaggerated that it is amazing to think people believed them; it seemed rather like a modern-day Promised Land, flowing with milk and honey.

Long before the pioneers reached Oregon, industrious white men saw the territory was rich with fur pelts. During the early 1800s, John Jacob Astor planned to set up trading posts in the vast western land and build a large settlement along the Columbia River where his company could trap and trade for furs. Soon a race began between Astor's Pacific Fur Company and the British Hudson Bay Company to be the first to establish a fort in Oregon. Triumphantly, the Americans arrived in Oregon aboard the

Tonquin in 1811 and set up a post they dubbed Fort Astoria in honor of their founder.

These early mountain men paved the way for future settlements by Americans. Robert Stuart, one of Astor's partners, discovered a route over the Rocky Mountains in October of 1812 when he crossed the Great Divide at South Pass in present-day Wyoming. This discovery seemed insignificant at the time, but soon became valuable as the easiest pass through the Rocky Mountains.

As reports of Oregon reached the east, missionaries became interested in serving there. A story was widely circulated in the east about four Indians who had traveled from Oregon to St. Louis to seek the "White Man's Book of Heaven." Although some claim that the story was fictional, it helped missionaries to see Oregon as a spiritually hungry place, and they began setting up missions in the new territory. In 1836, Dr. Marcus Whitman, his wife Narcissa, Reverend Henry Spalding, and his wife Eliza, left the comforts of the east to minister in Oregon. Narcissa and Eliza were the first white women to cross the Continental Divide. Their journey proved that women, and thus whole families, could travel overland to Oregon.

An economic depression that took place in the late 1830s, called the Panic of 1837, lead countless emigrants to seek new land in Oregon. Many people longed for a fresh start, and the vivid tales of Oregon were just what their itching ears wanted to hear. Oregon promised fertile soil and a pleasant climate. During the following years, a few pioneers reached this alleged Promised Land, but in 1843, the Great Migration began. A wagon train with one thousand emigrants and one hundred and twenty wagons headed west. Thus begins the history of the Oregon Trail, which vibrantly lives as one of the greatest chapters in American history.

The road to Oregon was hard, long, and dangerous. Attempting to cross over two thousand miles of seemingly endless prairies, perilous rivers, and rugged mountains was not for the fainthearted.

Another daunting fear was the possibility of attacks by Native Americans. In the early years of the Trail, Indians were very helpful to emigrants; they served as guides and willingly traded supplies with the pioneers. As time passed, however, the relationship between the Indians and pioneers deteriorated, and conflicts became more frequent. Most of the deaths on the trail, however, were caused by accidents or diseases, such as dysentery, cholera, and scurvy.

Every day the pioneers faced situations that could be fatal—river crossings, poisonous snakes, unsanitary water, attacks from wild animals, and storms. Approximately three hundred thousand people traveled on the Oregon Trail from 1840–1860, and it is estimated that thirty-four thousand emigrants perished.

THE OREGON TRAIL

Pioneers who wished to reach to Oregon traveled from their homes in the east to jump-off points along the Oregon Trail. The most well-known was Independence, Missouri. During the spring, the city would be bustling with the noises of wagon trains preparing to start their six-month journey. Meticulously, families loaded their sturdy Conestoga wagons with food, tools, supplies, and household necessities. Each family would need about one thousand dollars to buy provisions. To keep off the sun and weather, the wagons were covered with strong white canvases that reminded people of ships, and the wagons were nicknamed *prairie schooners*. When choosing animals to pull the wagons, most pioneers went with oxen, as they were strong, sturdy, good-tempered (unlike donkeys), and could live off the land.

Once their provisions were purchased and the wagons loaded, the eager pioneers started their tedious journey, usually in April or May. In the beginning, everything seemed like a fantastic adventure, but it soon became a monotonous routine. At four o'clock in the morning, the watchman fired his rifle to announce a new day. While the men yoked the oxen and reloaded the wagons, the women-folk lit fires and cooked their breakfast of coffee, bacon, and johnnycakes. On the prairie, trees were scarce, and they used buffalo chips (dried buffalo droppings) in place of firewood.

At seven o'clock in the morning, the pilot or wagon master blew a trumpet or bugle to get the wagons started. If a wagon was slow to get in its assigned position, it had to ride at the back of the wagon train, and it would soon be covered with dust. Each day the wagon in front was changed, so every family had a chance to be free from the dust of the other wagons.

At noon, they stopped for the midday meal, which consisted of leftovers from breakfast. During "nooning," the animals were given a much-needed hour's rest. Continuing their journey, they stopped at six o'clock in the evening to make camp. The wagons were placed in a circle and attached together using the oxen's chains. The area inside the circle was used as the campground and also gave the pioneers protection. Soon a crackling fire was blazing and a dinner of rice and beans or bacon, bread, and occasionally a pie, was prepared.

By nine o'clock, a quiet settled over the weary wagon train. As they slipped into an exhausted slumber, the fatigues of the day disappeared, and they would be refreshed when morning came. Each day was much like the last.

The early pioneers relied on landmarks to determine their progress and assure them they were on the right track. An average of twelve to fifteen miles was traveled each day. Whenever possible, they followed major rivers such as the North Platte, Sweetwater, Snake, and Columbia. This allowed them to have a constant water supply, but when it was impossible to follow a river, they suffered greatly from thirst. Some major landmarks along the Trail included Courthouse Rock, Chimney Rock, Fort Laramie, Register Cliff, Independence Rock, South Pass, Soda Springs, and Fort Hall.

Once the pioneers reached their Promised Land, the Willamette Valley, they began the grueling work of cutting logs to make shelters for themselves and their animals before winter set in.

The men, women, and children who traveled the Oregon Trail probably never realized that their sacrifices and hardships would be remembered almost two centuries later. In a harsh and vast wilderness, they marked out a trail that was followed by thousands of other enterprising pioneers. Soon, the number of Americans living in Oregon outnumbered the British. The Oregon Treaty of 1846 set the Canadian border at the forty-ninth parallel, thus making Oregon a U.S. territory.

In 1859, Oregon joined the Union as the thirty-third state. The daring pioneers who settled in Oregon had found their Promised Land, a place of fertile soil with delightful surroundings. Through their bravery and perseverance, they carved a home out of the wilderness.

Digging Deeper

How many miles long was the Oregon Trail?

How long did it take to go from Independence, Missouri, to the Willamette Valley?

What year did the Great Migration begin?

What were the wagons that the pioneers used called?

Play the computer game *Oregon Trail* and keep a journal of the events that happen during your trip. Write a short story about your journey to Oregon.

Read *The Oregon Tail* by Dana Meachen Rau. This book takes an in-depth look at everyday life on the trail.

Find out how the emigrants ate on the Oregon Trail by reading *Skillet Bread, Sourdough, and Vinegar Pie* by Loretta Frances Ichord. Then make one of the recipes in the book to experience a pioneer meal.

Sometimes it is hard to know what landmarks along the Oregon Trail looked like from a written description. *The Oregon Trail: A Photographic Journey* by Bill and Jan Moeller, has color photographs of the Trail and quotes from pioneer diaries. This book is a must for Oregon Trail study.

Chapter 18

The Pony Express
Uniting the East and West

A lone rider appears on the horizon. Every fiber of horse and man is straining toward the west. Steadily they come closer, until they pass by as quick as a flash of lightning. They are soon lost from view as they pursue the land of the setting sun.

In the mid-1860s, a mail service known as the Pony Express bridged the gap between east and west. Although the Pony Express only lasted eighteen months, it is a fascinating chapter in America's history.

The need for transcontinental mail service began in the 1840s, when pioneers began to settle in Oregon and gold was discovered in California. In 1850, California joined the Union, and Oregon followed in 1859. By 1860, the population in California was 380,000. As friction between north and south intensified, the western states wanted to stay up to date on these events. In 1856, 75,000 people from California signed a petition requesting that the government improve the mail service between the east and west. At the time, it took up to six months for mail to reach the west.

When the government proposed a plan for upgrading the mail service, the deep-rooted conflict between north and south again reared its ugly head. Both sides wanted the mail route to go through their part of the country. Since the Postmaster General, Aaron W. Brown, was from the south, he approved the southern route that went through Texas, New Mexico, and Arizona. Known as the Butterfield Route, it was seven hundred miles longer than the northern route and went through very hostile Indian country. It took twenty-five days to get the stagecoaches with the mail from Little Rock, Arkansas, to California.

Clearly, there had to be a faster way to get the mail west. The idea for the Pony Express came from William H. Russell after a conversation with California senator William M. Gwin. While in Washington getting contracts for the freight company of Russell, Majors, and Waddell, Russell formed the plan of creating a mail service using lightweight riders and fast horses. His partners, Alexander H. Majors and William B. Waddell, were not enthusiastic about his scheme, but they agreed to go along with it.

Senator Gwin was hopeful of getting a government contract to finance the venture. Unfortunately, this did not happen. The plans went ahead anyway, and Russell had just sixty-five days to have everything ready in time for their first ride, scheduled for April 3. There were many preparations to be made. Every twelve to fifteen miles, a relay station had to be built. Five hundred fast horses had to be purchased, eighty skilled riders had to be found, and two hundred station managers needed to be hired.

One of the most critical parts of the Pony Express was the rider. The following advertisement appeared in newspapers: "WANTED. Young, skinny, wiry fellows not over 18. Must be expert riders, willing to risk death daily. Orphans preferred. Wages $25 a week."

From the hundreds who applied, eighty riders were selected. Each rider received a Bible and took an oath not to fight, swear, or drink alcohol. They promised to be honest and faithful in their duties. Although most riders were in their teens, the youngest was only eleven years old, and some of the men were in their forties.

On April 3, 1860, the first westbound rider departed from St. Joseph, Missouri, and the first eastbound rider left San Francisco. In both cities, the first run of the Pony Express was celebrated by speech making and bands playing. The riders wore red shirts and carried two Colt revolvers, one Spencer rifle, and a bugle to announce their arrival at the relay stations.

The terrain from St. Joseph was mostly prairie and made for easy riding, but the eastbound riders had to cross the daunting Sierra Nevada Mountains on the first leg of the journey. Snow and avalanches could not stop the Pony Express. "The mail must go through!" was their motto. In ten days the riders arrived on the other side of the continent. The first run of the Pony Express was a success!

The Pony Express riders were heralded as heroes in newspapers across the land, but their true bravery was evident in the steadfast way they delivered the mail from St. Joseph to Sacramento. The Pony Express route covered two thousand miles of rough country. It followed the Overland or Oregon Trail for the first part of the journey. After South Pass, the Pony Express headed southwest for Salt Lake, and then it crossed another dry prairie before reaching the Sierra Nevada Mountains. In all kinds of weather, twenty-four hours a day, those courageous men were in the saddle carrying the mail.

"The mail first, horse second, and rider last," was an unwritten code that the riders followed. Their bright red shirts were replaced with sturdy buckskins, the bugle was abandoned, and the riders limited their weapons to one Colt revolver and an extra cylinder of ammunition to help lighten their load. Special saddles were made for the Pony Express: a cross between a western and a jockey saddle.

Over the saddle was placed a mochila (pronounced m-CHEE-la), which was made of leather and contained four pockets. Three pockets were locked, and the fourth held mail that was delivered along the trail. When letters were sent through the Pony Express, they were written on thin tissue paper and then wrapped in oiled silk for protection.

A month after the first run, a war broke out between the Paiute Indians and the settlers in the area of Nevada. In May 1860, several relay stations were attacked near Carson City. Being a station manager was a dangerous job, much more so than being a rider. If Indians or bandits attacked a rider, he relied on his horse to outrun his pursuers; but the men at the stations were practically sitting ducks. Several station managers were killed during the Paiute War. The Pony Express temporarily stopped operations until the Paiutes were subdued. In June 1860, after three weeks, the Pony Express began to run again.

While the riders were facing bandits, Indians, wild animals, harsh terrain, and severe weather, the owners were confronting financial difficulties. Initially, the price to mail a letter was five dollars, but it slowly dropped to one dollar by July 1861. For each letter the Pony Express carried, they were spending $16. The Paiute War cost Russell, Majors, and Waddell $75,000.

In December 1860, Russell embezzled $870,000 in bonds from the Interior Department. Never intending to keep the bonds, Russell merely planned to use them as collateral to get a bank loan. After the loan had been repaid, he intended to return the bonds. When his act was discovered, Russell was imprisoned. However, in January 1861, he was acquitted.

Regardless of what his motives may have been, his wrong actions did not help the credibility of the Pony Express. Its official name was the Central Overland California and Pikes Peak Express, but people began referring to it as the Clean Out of Cash and Poor Pay

Express. If the Pony Express had received a million-dollar contract from the government it might have saved the company, but instead the contract went to John Butterfield, who had delivered the mail through the southern route that bore his name. To add insult to injury, Butterfield was also given permission to use the same route that the Pony Express followed. For a while, the Pony Express and Butterfield teamed up, but by the time the transcontinental telegraph was completed on October 24, 1861, the Pony Express was nearing the end. Two days later it ceased operations.

When the Pony Express began, Russell, Majors, and Waddell were prosperous businessmen, but when it ended they were bankrupt. They lost $200,000 in the venture. Natural forces could not stop the Pony Express; it was financial troubles that led to its demise.

The Pony Express helped keep California and Oregon in the Union when southern states were leaving it. It was the Pony Express that delivered the results of Lincoln's victory in the 1860 Election. In a daring feat, the Pony Express carried Lincoln's inaugural address in March of 1861 to California in an astounding seven days and seventeen hours. During its short-lived existence, the Pony Express served as a uniting force in a country that was strongly divided.

Digging Deeper

Who started the Pony Express?

What was the purpose of the Pony Express?

Make a time line of the Pony Express from the information in this chapter, or, for a more in-depth time line, consult a book such as the one listed below. Include information about other events that were happening in the United States around the same time—for example, the start of the Civil War.

Read *The Pony Express: A Photographic History* by Bill and Jan Moeller. This book traces the actual trail that the Pony Express used.

Examine a map of the route followed by the Pony Express. The book referred to above has a map.

Chapter 19

A Tale of Two Generals
Biographies of General Lee & General Grant

During the 1860s, two generals stepped into the history books and left an undeniable mark on the United States of America. In many ways they were similar. They both graduated from West Point, married into slave-holding families, fought in the Mexican War, and were incredible military leaders. Who were these men? Robert E. Lee and Ulysses S. Grant, of course.

Robert E. Lee

In October of 1862, Robert E. Lee went through his mail. He gave the necessary orders to his secretary. When the secretary left, Lee finally gave vent to his unbearable grief. A letter had come telling of his favorite daughter Annie's death. Although Lee saw hundreds of thousands of men die in the War Between the States, it was the loss of his precious daughter that caused the general of the Confederate States to cry.

In this trial, as in many others, Lee found comfort from God. In a letter to his wife he said, "But God in this, as in all things, has mingled mercy with the blow in selecting that one best prepared to leave us." Putting his own grief

109

aside, Lee won a decisive victory at Fredericksburg only a few months later. His magnificent leadership and strong Christian beliefs pulled him and the South through four years of bloody civil war.

When the War Between the States began, Lee was offered the command of the United States Army. Whether to join the North or the South was the most difficult decision Lee ever made. Personally, he disapproved of slavery and secession. Loyalty to Virginia determined his fate, however, and when she seceded he joined the Southern cause. "Trusting in Almighty God . . . I devote myself to the service of my native State, in whose behalf alone will I ever again draw my sword," he said at the Virginia convention. Even the name of his army showed what he was fighting for: it was the Army of Northern Virginia

In 1862, Union forces under General McClellan marched toward Richmond intending to end the rebellion in one crushing blow. What they didn't count on was Robert E. Lee! During the Seven Days' Battle around Richmond, Lee and his men won great victories against the invaders. The South was elated, and Lee was dubbed the "Savior of Richmond."

Lee and the South marked the early years of the war with brilliant victories. Lee was a born leader. He cared for his men, never putting himself above them, and they always respected his authority. Time after time he showed his kindness and love for his men, but when he was disobeyed, he could inflict harsh discipline. In many ways he resembled George Washington, whom he admired. Through sheer genius, Lee outwitted one Union general after another. Even with fewer supplies than the North, Lee always managed to gain the upper hand.

In the summer of 1863 Lee invaded the North, intending to capture Philadelphia. At the battle of Gettysburg (July 1–3, 1863), Lee was so confident in his men that he expected them to perform almost supernatural feats. They almost did! In the end, however, Lee was forced to retreat. Finally he faced an opponent who was worthy of him: Ulysses S. Grant.

In 1864 Lee led several devastating attacks on Grant's troops as they headed South. Although the Wilderness Campaigns cost many Union lives, Grant did not retreat. After every battle, including the victories, Lee lost men who could not be replaced. The Army of Northern Virginia never had enough food, ammunition, clothing, or medical supplies, but they stayed and fought because of Lee. Affectionately they called him "Marse Robert."

Lee and his men were finally trapped in Petersburg, where Grant kept them under siege during much of 1864–65. Feeling the end creeping nearer, Lee was disheartened when Richmond fell on April 3, 1865.

One last hope remained for the South. If Lee and his men could slip out of Petersburg and head south to join Joe Johnston in North Carolina, maybe they could still strike a decisive blow at the enemy. Although they did leave Petersburg, they were defeated. Robert E. Lee surrendered to Grant on April 9, 1865.

With the coming of peace, Lee helped bring the two sides back together. On April 14, 1865, he said, "Go home and take up any work that offers. Accept conditions as you find them. Consider only the present and future. Do not cherish bitterness." His example of forgiveness inspired others. After the war, the hero was offered many positions, and in August of 1865 he became the president of Washington College in Lexington, Virginia. His years at the college were some of the happiest of his life.

In the late 1860s Lee began experiencing heart problems, and on October 12, 1870, the illustrious general died.

A Quick Overview of Robert Edward Lee

Personal appearance: Five feet eleven inches tall; 170 pounds; hair black when young and gray later in life; eyes brown.

Born: January 19, 1807

Parents: Henry "Light-Horse Harry" Lee, Revolutionary War general, and Ann Hill Carter Lee

Education: Graduated from West Point in 1829, second in his class. Robert E. Lee is the only person to make it through West Point with no demerits!

Wife: Mary Anne Custis Lee (1808–1873), the great-granddaughter of Martha Washington

Date of marriage: June 30, 1831

Children: George Washington Custis (called Custis), Mary, William Henry Fitzhugh (called Rooney), Annie, Agnes, Robert E. Lee Jr., and Mildred

Died: October 12, 1870

~~Quotes~~

"It is well that war is so terrible—otherwise we should grow too fond of it." – at the Battle of Fredericksburg

"Duty is the sublimest word in our language. Do your duty in all things. You cannot do more. You should never wish to do less." – to his son, G. W. Custis Lee

Ulysses S. Grant

Ulysses S. Grant was one of the least likely boys in all of Ohio to make a name for himself. When he was a child, he was so awkward and uncertain that people called him "Useless" instead of Ulysses. This seemingly worthless lad would grow up to lead one of the greatest armies of all time and save the Union.

Because of his indecisiveness, Grant's parents sent him to West Point, hoping he would pursue a military career. He did join the army, and during the Mexican War, Grant's clever mind showed true military genius. After the war, he was sent all over the country from New York to Washington to California. Missing his family, he resigned from the army and tried many different jobs. He attempted farming, working as a rent collector, and later serving as a clerk. Nothing suited him. Despite his failures, when the Civil War began, Grant finally found his place in the world and was made colonel of the Twenty-First Illinois Regiment.

Grant showed talent that seemed to be lacking in so many Union officers. He knew how to handle his men and always led by example. His honest manners and willingness to endure the same hardships as his men earned him their respect. After the victory at Vicksburg, Grant was promoted to a major general.

On April 6, 1862, Grant was surprised by a Confederate attack at Shiloh (Pittsburgh Landing). By nightfall the battle looked like a Union defeat, but reinforcements arrived headed by Lew Wallace, and the next day Grant was victorious. It had been a costly victory in which 13,000 Northern soldiers and 10,700 Southern soldiers had perished. President Lincoln saw that Grant was a good military leader, and he offered Grant the command of the entire Union army.

Knowing the tremendous responsibility he was taking, Grant said, "I feel the full weight of the responsibilities now devolving on me; and I know that if they are met, it will be due to those armies, and above all, to the favor of that Providence which leads both nations and men." Grant would do his best, but the outcome would be in God's hands. With this in mind, Grant grimly marched to Virginia.

In the wilderness, Grant was attacked by Lee. His men suffered terribly, with 17,666 casualties compared to the 7,750 casualties of the Confederates. People in the North called Grant a butcher and demanded his replacement, but Lincoln knew Grant wouldn't quit until the job was done. He knew that if he could keep the pressure on long enough, the war would end.

To accomplish this, Grant marched to Petersburg, intending to cut off Lee's supplies from the south and west. Lee reached Petersburg first. Until April 9, 1865, Grant kept hounding the Confederates. After the surrender, Grant stopped his men from rejoicing. He told them, "The war is over. The Rebels are our countrymen again."

In the North, Grant was welcomed as a hero, and he served two terms as president from 1869–1877. When he learned that he had throat cancer, he began writing his memoirs, knowing the sales would provide for his family. He finished the book one month before he died on July 23, 1885.

Lee and Grant were two of the greatest Americans of all time. They each used their God-given abilities to fight for what they held dear. They respected and admired each other for their military leadership.

A Quick Overview of Ulysses S. Grant

Personal appearance: Five feet eight inches; 135 pounds; hair brown; eyes gray-blue

Born: April 27, 1822

Parents: Jesse Root Grant and Hannah Simpson Grant

Education: Graduated from West Point in 1843, twenty-first in his class.

Wife: Julia Dent Grant (1826–1902)

Date of marriage: August 22, 1848

Children: Frederick Dent, Ulysses S. Grant Jr., Ellen Wrenshall, Jesse Root Grant Jr.

Died: July 23, 1885

~Quotes~

"The art of war is simple enough. Find out where your enemy is. Get at him as soon as you can. Strike him as hard as you can, and keep moving on."

"Though I have been trained as a soldier, and participated in many battles, there never was a time when, in my opinion, some way could not be found to prevent the drawing of the sword."

Digging Deeper

Make a list of Civil War battles.

Read Virginia's General by Albert Marrin and *Ulysses S. Grant* by Brenda Haugen.

Look up Lew Wallace in an encyclopedia. What famous book did he write?

Study a particular battle and then recreate it. Use beads for the soldiers and blankets and pillows to make the landscape. Toothpicks with bits of paper telling the different regiment names could serve as flags.

Chapter 20

The Spanish-American War

Few campaigns in America's history enjoyed more popularity than the Spanish-American War. For a few months during the summer of 1898, the United States lived all the romantic vigor that is associated with war. Tales of the daring actions of soldiers and sailors were celebrated with the utmost enthusiasm. This often-overlooked conflict did much to establish America as a world power.

The causes of the war began on the small island of Cuba. Since the days of Columbus this island had been ruled by Spain, but in the mid-1800s, the Cubans revolted against their masters. This conflict ended in 1878, when Spain promised to reform, but their oaths were empty. Those who had participated in the uprising were hunted down, and many escaped to the United States.

In 1895, Cuba again tried to gain her independence. Small bands of Cuban guerrillas wreaked havoc on the Spanish troops. Ruthlessly, Spain turned every part of the island into a war zone when General Weyler was sent to subdue the rebellion. Peasants were sent to concentration camps and farms were destroyed. The general was called "Butcher Weyler," and understandably so. During his rule, one fourth of the population, or about four hundred thousand people, perished. The Cubans' fight for freedom against the general's cruel tactics earned the sympathy of America.

Compassion alone was not enough to warrant American intervention. The United States' involvement in the war was largely due to the "yellow press." Fifteen years earlier, newspapers had changed from being purely informative to entertaining. They carried shocking stories, crossword puzzles, and also comic strips. The most famous was *The Yellow Kid*, and from there comes the term "yellow press."

Tales of Butcher Weyler's atrocities increased newspaper circulation, and the *New York Journal's* owner, William Randolph Hearst, wanted to keep the stories coming. He sent artist Fredric Remington to Cuba to draw pictures of the events. When Remington reported that things were peaceful, Hearst told him, "You furnish the pictures, and I'll furnish the war." Hearst's stories, often exaggerated, swayed public opinion, and people began clamoring for war.

The yellow press was ever looking for a juicy story, and in February of 1898, Hearst published a letter from the Spanish ambassador, Dupuy de Lôme. A Cuban spy had photographed the letter and sent it to Hearst. In the De Lôme Letter, as it was called, the Spanish ambassador said President McKinley was "weak and a bidder for the admiration of the crowd." This insult to their president further inflamed America.

On February 15, 1898, an event occurred that changed everything. The battleship *Maine* had been sent to Havana to protect American citizens and their property from riots. At 9:40 in the evening, the *Maine* exploded. The unexpected event left two hundred and sixty men dead. Only ninety sailors survived. Vehemently, the yellow press blamed Spain! Although the real cause of the *Maine's* explosion has never been solved, it is very unlikely that

Spain would have sought hostilities with America. After the explosion, Spanish sailors helped rescue the survivors of the wreck, and the dead were buried with Spanish military honors. However, America was ripe for war, and the sinking of the *Maine* pushed them into action. "Remember the *Maine!*" became the battle cry.

Reluctantly, President McKinley asked Congress to declare war. On April 25, 1898, they did. In the Pacific Ocean, Commodore George Dewey was waiting at Hong Kong for orders to attack the Spanish fleet if war was declared. On May 1, Dewey engaged the ancient Spanish fleet at the Battle of Manila Bay. The American ships were superior to those of the Spaniards, and without the loss of a single American, the Spanish fleet was destroyed.

The campaign in Cuba was not as easily won. Initially, an army had to be collected, outfitted, and trained. With fewer than 30,000 men in the army, McKinley called for 125,000 volunteers to fill the ranks. Among the volunteers were Theodore Roosevelt and the company he helped raise, the First United States Volunteer Cavalry, or the Rough Riders as they called themselves. They were a diverse group, from wealthy athletic men like Roosevelt, to hearty cowboys, sheriffs, and outlaws Teddy had met at his ranch in the Dakota Territory. Through Roosevelt's influence, the Rough Riders were given the best weapons and uniforms. They were the finest unit in the army.

Unfortunately, the rest of the military was in a state of disorder. Food supplies were a disgrace and the transportation of the troops a mess. Many soldiers were left behind because there were too few transports. Nearly half of the Rough Riders never saw action. When it appeared that the Rough Riders might be left behind, Teddy took matters into his own hands. He flagged down a train that took them to the embankment, and then he and his men commandeered the *Yucatán* to transport them to Cuba.

Departing on June 14, 1898, the fleet of crowded transports headed for Cuba with 15,058 men.

On June 22, the transports landed at Daiquiri and Siboney. A former Confederate general, Fightin' Joe Wheeler, ordered Old Glory hoisted on the hilltop. Two days later a battle was fought at Las Guásimas. The Spaniards were better equipped than the Americans. While most of the American soldiers had Springfield rifles, the Spanish were armed with a powderless gun called a Mauser. From their unknown position, the Spanish kept the Americans pinned down. Eventually, Richard Harding Davis located the enemy, and the Rough Riders, who were armed with Kragg rifles, returned fire. Soon the Spaniards retreated.

The Spanish fleet under Admiral Pascual Cervera lay in Santiago Bay. Earlier in the war, the yellow press had frightened the American people into thinking that the Spanish fleet would attack the United States. Two navy squadrons were sent to find and destroy the Spanish fleet. After they sailed around the Gulf of Mexico, they found the Spaniards at Santiago Bay in Cuba. The city's defenses made it impossible for the Americans to attack, so they set up a blockade. On June 3, 1898, the Americans tried to sink the *Merrimac* at the mouth of the bay to prevent Cervera from leaving. Unfortunately, the *Merrimac* did not explode, and the plan was unsuccessful.

Along the San Juan Ridge, the Spanish had built a line of defenses, with strongholds at San Juan Hill, Kettle Hill, and El Caney. Before the Americans could attack Santiago, they had to take these key positions. The plan of attack was not very well thought-out by the leader of the Americans, Major General Shafter. He sent his troops along a narrow jungle trail to reach the Spanish embankment. From the heights above, the Spanish delivered a deadly fire into the advancing troops on July 1, 1898.

When they finally reached Kettle Hill, the men waited for orders to attack. It seemed they were to stay there forever, just waiting for the Spanish to pick them off, when suddenly three Gatling guns arrived and began pouring bullets into the Spanish ranks. Without orders, Lieutenant Jules Ord led his men up the hill. Once they began moving, the rest followed. At San Juan Hill, the Rough Riders led the charge. Teddy was the only one with a mount; the other horses had been left in Florida. The vigor of the American soldiers soon won the victory. America had 205 killed and 1,180 wounded, while Spain suffered 215 deaths and 375 wounded.

After the victories at San Juan Hill and Kettle Hill, the Cuban governor ordered Cervera's fleet to leave Santiago. He wished to save the fleet if possible. Getting past the blockade was impossible, and the ensuing battle led to another victory for the United States.

Spain was defeated. On July 27, 1898, a cease-fire took place to begin peace talks. At this point, another enemy began attacking the U.S. soldiers—yellow fever. Over three thousand men were sick with the disease on July 28, and the number kept rising. If the troops were not moved from the deadly climate, soon thousands would die.

On August 7, the troops were sent back to the United States. The peace treaty was signed on December 10, 1898. Over three hundred men had been killed, but the real tragedy of the Spanish-American War was the 5,462 men who died of diseases and poor sanitation both in Cuban and U.S. camps.

The Spanish-American War—although only four months in length—helped propel the United States into the twentieth century as a rising world power. It also helped heal the wounds still left over from the Civil War by giving the nation—both North and South—a common military objective for the first time since the War Between the States.

John Hay, the American ambassador to England, summed up the American sentiment of the time when he said it was "a splendid little war."

Digging Deeper

In what year did the Spanish-American War take place?

What was the name of the most well-known regiment of the war?

Read the complete De Lôme letter at
www.ourdocuments.gov/doc.php?doc=53

The Spanish-American War by Kerry A. Graves would be a good book for younger children, while *The Spanish-American War* by Albert Marrin is suitable for high school students. (Caution: This book contains some quotes with bad language.)

Look up Cuba in an encyclopedia and research the island's history and geography. Then write a short report from the information you learn.

Chapter 21

The Klondike Gold Rush

"GOLD! GOLD IN THE KLONDIKE! BRIGHT SHINY GOLD!" That was the news the steamship *Excelsior* brought to the world when it arrived in San Francisco in mid-July of 1897. Seattle bustled with excitement the next day when the *Portland* docked and proclaimed the same news. Between these two boats were eighty miners and three tons of gold.

The tales of gold, which flooded the newspapers, fascinated many people. Suddenly everyone wanted to know where the Klondike was and how to get there. The Klondike, located just east of the Alaskan border, comes from the Indian word *Thron-diuck* meaning "the place where fishnets are hung on stakes." People read articles about the Klondike, talked about it with friends, and dreamed of journeying to the gold fields to make their fortunes.

The First Prospectors

The summer before, three friends, George Carmack (called Siwash George), Skookum Jim, and Dawson Charlie were fishing in the Klondike area when they

123

discovered gold. Alaska and the Yukon Territory had long been the home of wandering prospectors called "sourdoughs." Before these three friends found gold, they were visited by Robert Henderson, who said he had found gold in a creek not far away, and Henderson welcomed George to come and prospect with him but said the Indians (Skookum Jim and Dawson Charlie) could not join him. Clearly, this offended the friends, so the three stayed at Rabbit Creek. One day they pulled up three dollars' worth of gold in one pan. What a find! While George and Charlie went to Fortymile to stake their claims, Jim remained at the creek to guard their discovery.

Once news spread of the strike, a mad rush was made by the sourdoughs from all over Alaska and the Yukon. When the miners realized the vast amount of gold Rabbit Creek contained, they renamed it Bonanza Creek. In Spanish, *bonanza* means "rich with wealth or gold." A tributary of Bonanza Creek proved even more loaded with "color." It was dubbed Eldorado, after a legendary city of gold in South America. Eldorado was the richest stream in the world! Patiently, the miners worked throughout the long, frigid, dark winter.

Rushing to the Gold Fields

Once the world knew about the Klondike, thousands of hearty people began a stampede to the area. Many difficulties arose for those wishing to go. The fee for passage in a ship was fifteen hundred dollars, and each person was allowed to bring twelve hundred pounds of supplies. To survive in the Klondike for eighteen months, a person needed half a ton of provisions. During the years of 1897–1898, one hundred thousand people set out for the Klondike, but because of the hardships, only fifty thousand ever made it. Traveling from the ports on the west coast of North America, those with "Klondike Fever" landed at

Skagway or Dyea, the first and easiest part of their journey completed.

Many natural barriers stood in their way to the gold fields, the first of which was the Coast Mountains. There were two different trails that led through the vast mountains: the Skagway Trail and Dyea Trail. Skagway Trail, a forty-five mile trek, reached a height of twenty-nine hundred feet above sea level at White Pass. Dyea Trail was only thirty-three miles long, but just as arduous. On this trail, the mountains were crossed at Chilkoot Pass, where individuals would carry packs of seventy-five to one hundred pounds on their backs up the fifteen hundred steps chiseled out of the frozen snow. Most people carried their provisions; they would haul a load for a mile and then return to get another load. It was a time-consuming process.

At both Chilkoot Pass and White Pass, the Canadian Mounted Police inspected their supplies. If an individual had over five hundred dollars and one year of provisions, they were allowed to continue. If not, they were told to go back.

The Bottom of Chilkoot Pass

After White Pass, they reached Lake Lindeman, and those who crossed Chilkoot Pass arrived at Lake Bennett. From these lakes, boats were constructed to float down the Yukon River. Finally, the spring of 1898 emerged, and with it the thaw of the Yukon River. Sailing the five hundred and fifty miles to Dawson and the gold fields, the fortune hunters' journey was nearly finished. The only difficulty on the river happened at Miles Canyon, where a constant whirlpool trapped many boats and sent their passengers to a watery grave.

The Cheechakos Arrive

Joyfully, the greenhorns, or *cheechakos,* as they were called, reached Dawson. Already the city was a thriving metropolis with seven restaurants, two butcher shops, four stores, two banks, two newspapers, a hospital, and a telephone line (which only worked in Dawson!). The prices at Dawson were incredible. A gallon of milk sold for thirty dollars, a dozen eggs for fourteen dollars, and a kitten for fifteen dollars. Many of the newcomers returned home immediately, while the more hearty ones began panning for the beckoning gold. The Mounties maintained law and order in Dawson, making it a very different town from other gold rush cities.

During the summer of 1898, the newcomers began digging for gold. In July, more than nine thousand claims were registered. Diligently, they dug the solid land. Fires were lit on the ground to soften the frozen earth. All through the long winter of 1898–1899, sourdoughs and *cheechakos* dug for the precious metal.

Klondike Missionaries

Several missionaries served the miners in the Klondike. There was Father Judge, a Jesuit missionary who opened a hospital called St. Mary's, where he cared for those sick with malaria, pneumonia, bronchitis, and scurvy. Known as "The Saint of Dawson," he also built a church, and when it

126

burned down the people of Dawson helped him rebuild. Sadly, Father Judge died of pneumonia shortly after the Christmas of 1898. The entire city mourned for him. It took the men two and a half days to dig his grave in the frozen ground.

Another missionary was Bishop Bompas from the Church of England, who along with his wife had been serving the Indians in the area before the gold rush. Hall Young represented the Presbyterian Church, along with Reverend George A. McEwen, who helped him establish a church. Their church also burned down, but the hearty members found another building where they could worship. Contrary to what you might expect, no work was conducted on Sundays in Dawson.

Changes in Dawson

The temperature was a cold, forty-five degrees below zero on the night of April 20, 1899, when a fire broke out in a saloon. Soon, a large part of the town blazed in flames and a million dollars worth of property was destroyed. The following summer, many improvements were made during the rebuilding of Dawson. Although much gold still remained in the ground by the summer of 1899, Dawson and the Klondike's days of glory were fading. Large companies with machinery took control. Many sourdoughs left to search for gold elsewhere, while those who had struck it rich settled down. The Klondike produced many wealthy people. Each of the original forty claims made half a million dollars, which in today's value would be about seven million dollars.

Famous Klondike Citizens

Several famous people emerged from the Klondike Gold Rush. Augustus Mack returned to his New York home and started a factory making Mack trucks. Belinda Mulroney, already a successful businesswoman because of her ownership of the Fairview Hotel in Dawson, became even more prominent as the manager of the largest gold mining company in the Klondike. The three men who first discovered gold all became wealthy. Regrettably, George Carmack left his Indian wife and married a white woman before he settled down to a life of ease. Dawson Charlie purchased a hotel and managed it successfully. Skookum Jim spent his life searching for more and more gold, never satisfied with his large fortune.

By the middle of 1899, the gold rush that caused such frenzy had ended. The Klondike Gold Rush is remembered as an exciting, larger-than-life experience of the kind which only happens in storybooks. But it was true, and despite its short duration, was an amazing episode in history.

Digging Deeper

Define unfamiliar words such as *Eldorado, Bonanza, cheechakos*, etc.

Find Skagway, Dawson, Fortymile, and the Klondike on a map. The book listed below contains a map.

Read *The Alaska Gold Rush* by May McNeer. This book is easy to read and very interesting.

Seasoned miners were called *sourdoughs* because they loved to eat sourdough bread. Make a loaf yourself; *Alaska Sourdough* by Ruth Allman has many recipes. Another book that has sourdough starter is *Skillet Bread, Sourdough, and Vinegar Pie* by Loretta Frances Ichord.

Imagine you are a miner in the Klondike gold fields during the winter of 1898–1899. Write a letter home telling of your experiences.

Chapter 22

The Great War
America in the First World War

What happened at the eleventh hour of the eleventh day of the eleventh month in 1918? What war was labeled "the War to End All Wars" and "the Great War"? All too often World War I is eclipsed by World War II, but to fully understand the latter, the former must be studied because they are connected in many ways.

Before the Great War, Europe was a continent of powerful countries all vying for supremacy as world leaders. Fearing to be overshadowed, they formed strong alliances with other countries to increase their power. Great Britain, France, and Russia formed the Triple Entente, and Germany, Austria-Hungary, and Italy made up the Triple Alliance.

The strength of these alliances was tested when the heir of the Austria-Hungary throne, Archduke Franz Ferdinand, and his wife, Sophie, were assassinated in Sarajevo, Bosnia, on June 24, 1914. Bosnia, a province of Austria, wished to either be an independent country or ruled by their neighbor, Serbia. In Bosnia, a terrorist group called the Black Hand plotted to kill the Archduke Ferdinand, and it was one of their members, Gavrilo Princip, who succeeded in carrying out the plan.

Clearly, Serbia had influenced the assassin, and the infuriated Austrian government sent an ultimatum to Serbia demanding they comply with ten points to avoid war. Although Serbia agreed to most of the demands, they refused the two most important. Seeking assistance, Serbia appealed to their mighty friend, Russia.

On July 28, 1914, Austria declared war on Serbia. This action set off a chain of events: Russia declared war on Austria. Germany declared war against Russia on August 1, and two days later on France, an ally of Great Britain. On August 4, German troops marched across neutral Belgium on their way to France, bringing England into the war. When the battle lines were drawn up, there was Germany, Austria-Hungary, Bulgaria, and Turkey on the Central Powers side, and Great Britain, France, Russia, Belgium, Italy, Montenegro, Serbia, Japan, China, Portugal, Romania, and Greece on the Allied Powers side.

The United States watched for nearly three years as Europe tried to destroy itself. Wisely, President Woodrow Wilson proclaimed America a neutral country. Since immigrants from all parts of Europe lived in America, there were groups who sympathized with both sides.

Seeing the Central Powers' aggressive tactics in Belgium, the United States' allegiance began moving in the direction of the Allies. This was heightened when a German U-boat torpedoed a British passenger liner, the *Lusitania*, on May 7, 1915. Nearly two hundred Americans were on board, and over a hundred of them died, including millionaire Alfred Vanderbilt. Outraged, America demanded justice. Germany, however, was able to appease the United States for the time being by promising not to sink passenger ships in the future.

For a time, America's anger subsided. The war brought prosperity to the U.S. as the farmers and factories made goods to sell to Europe. America sold $3 billion worth of supplies and food to Britain, $1 billion to France, and $383 million to Germany.

In January 1917, the Germans began their U-boat attacks on neutral ships. Another event which helped end America's patience was the "Zimmermann Telegraph." The British intercepted a note from German foreign minister Arthur Zimmermann to the Mexican president. In the note, the Germans promised to return parts of the southwest that Mexico had lost during the Mexican War if Mexico would promise to enter into the war against the U.S. in the event America declared war on Germany. The American people were irate! Although President Wilson loved peace and had fought to keep the U.S. out of the war, he addressed Congress on April 2, 1917, asking them for a declaration of war. On April 6, America entered World War I.

A new mode of warfare greeted the American soldiers. Many improvements had been made in machinery. Successfully, the Germans used the U-boats (*unterseebooten*, meaning underwater boats) to destroy unsuspecting ships. Aircraft were also new to the scene. At first, airplanes were used for observation, but soon they became a new weapon. With a machine gun strapped to the front, pilots would engage in battles called "dog fights." The public loved the idea of brave pilots fighting in the sky and preferred those stories to the truth about life in the trenches.

Both sides had dug an extensive network of deep trenches in the ground. Instead of being a war of attack, this was one of defense. Running from the English Channel to Switzerland, the Western Front was nothing more than a line of trenches. Life in the trenches was terrible! Many times soldiers were up to their knees in water, and rats, lice, and other vermin were their constant companions. The area between the opposing sides' trenches was known as "no man's land," and anyone venturing into that area was mowed down with machine-gun fire. In April 1915, the Germans used a new weapon, poison gas (chlorine), and soon both sides were using it, making a gas mask a necessary addition to the soldier's uniform. Tanks were also introduced during World War I.

George M. Cohan's song "Over There" was sung as the first troops headed to France in the summer of 1917. America's army consisted of 4.8 million men who had either volunteered or been drafted. Preparing the doughboys (a nickname used for the Americans soldiers), the government set up military training camps. General John J. Pershing commanded the American Expeditionary Force.

Initially, the Americans filled up vacancies in the Allied ranks, but Pershing envisioned a united American army. His wish was granted in August 1918. Before that, however, on March 1, 1918, Russia signed a peace treaty with Germany. This meant that the German soldiers who had held the Eastern Front were able to be moved to the Western Front in the hopes of crushing the Allies before America could send enough men to oppose them.

Germany's lofty goal of reaching Paris failed at the Second Battle of the Marne. On July 15, 1918, the Germans made a concentrated effort to cross the Marne River in the Chateau-Thierry sector. Under the cover of darkness, the Germans threw shrapnel and poison gas into America's outnumbered Third Division. Many brave men fought fearlessly, but none as gallantly as the Thirty-Eighth Regiment. They were called "The Rock of the Marne" because only thirty-five hundred U.S. soldiers held their position against twenty thousand Germans!

Battles continued in several sectors until August 8, 1918, when the Germans were pushed back from the position they had held for four years. The First Battle of the Marne had begun on September 3, 1914, when the seemingly invincible Germans were pushing hard and fast toward Paris. Strangely, however, they had halted at the Marne. The Princess Pat Canadian Regiment said they saw a "man on a white horse" charging toward the German advance. General Gunn, the leader of the Princess Pat Regiment, commanded his soldiers to "follow the man on the white horse." Immediately, the Germans began marching the other direction, and the Allies went on the offense and drove the Germans back until the tenth of September.

Proclaiming Divine intervention, General Foch of France gave God all the glory for the event. Even the Germans consented that they lost the war when, for no apparent reason, they retreated at the First Battle of the Marne. Such amazing events can only happen by the powerful hand of God. Just as the First Battle of the Marne lifted the spirits of the Allies, so did the Second Battle, and it was the beginning of the end for Germany.

Several more months of fighting took place. The Allies claimed victories at the Battle of Saint-Mihiel and the Battle of the Argonne. Devastated Germany revolted against Kaiser Wilhelm II (called Kaiser Bill in America) and set up a socialistic government. A tired, defeated Germany finally asked for peace.

It was on the eleventh hour of the eleventh day of the eleventh month that an armistice was at last proclaimed. Joyfully, the world welcomed the coming of peace. Although President Wilson wrote "Fourteen Points" that he thought should appear in the final peace treaty, the other countries disagreed, and the final draft of the Treaty of Versailles put harsh conditions on the German people that made them ripe to follow a World War I veteran, Adolph Hitler, nearly twenty years later.

World War I was called "the War to End All Wars," but it seems a more appropriate title would be "the beginning of a century of wars." New technology made it easier to move troops, manufacture weapons, and carry on communications. Of the 65 million men who fought, over 8.5 million died and 21 million were wounded. America alone sacrificed 116,516 of her sons in the war.

It is interesting to think what might have occurred if the Allied forces had lost the war. What would have happened when the Nazis took control of Germany? There would have been no one to stop the horrors that led up to World War II if Europe had been under German control. In 1918, the world did not know of the coming storm; they only welcomed the glorious peace that had been purchased at a high price.

Digging Deeper

Which countries formed the Triple Entente and the Triple Alliance?

Name the countries that made up the Central Powers and the Allied Powers.

What were some new forms of weapons used in World War I?

Read *World War I: "The War to End Wars"* by Zachary Kent. This book gives an excellent overview of the war.

Look at a map of Europe before and after the war. The book mentioned above has these maps, as do most history books.

During the years between World War I and World War II, November 11 was celebrated as Armistice Day and later the name was changed to Veterans Day. Pretend you are a soldier and write a letter home telling your family how you feel on Armistice Day.

Chapter 23

The Legacy of Alvin York
American Hero of the First World War

Since World War I has been so overshadowed in history by World War II, it is, in a way, a forgotten war. As a result, it is also true that the heroes of this conflict have been lost in the pages of history. Every schoolchild once knew the names of valiant men who fought against the Central Powers. Their sacrifice, bravery, and loyalty equaled that of soldiers in any war.

The deeds and devotion of forgotten heroes are worthy of examination.

One of the Great War's most amazing heroes was Alvin C. York. Interestingly, he never wanted to be a soldier, and he abhorred bloodshed. When he was first drafted, York applied for an exemption, but the government rejected his appeal. If York's request had been granted, it is probable that the outcome of one battle would have been very different.

In October 1917, the Allied Powers penetrated the German lines. On the eighth of that month, Alvin C. York and the Eighty-Second Division (called the All-American Division because it was said there were men serving in the division from nearly every state) entered the German-infested Argonne Forest. Their objective was to destroy the Decauville Railroad and thus prevent supplies and troops from reaching the German line. First, however, they had to capture Hill 223, or Castle Hill as the Germans called it.

At 6:10 a.m. the Americans began their advance and were greeted by machine guns and poisonous gas. Stalled by the heavy fire, Sergeant Harry Parsons ordered seventeen men, including York, to crawl back through the underbrush to attack the hill from behind. Gradually, the Americans made their way toward the back of the hill. The Americans soon captured a group of German soldiers who were leisurely eating their breakfast.

When the German machine-gun operators saw the Americans to their rear, they turned the guns around and opened a deadly fire on the small group of Americans. The German prisoners hit the ground, and the Americans followed suit. Although the Americans sought shelter among the prisoners and behind trees or other brush, the Germans still managed to kill six and wound three, leaving York, who at that time was a corporal, in command. He had been caught in the open without any shelter while enemy bullets pelted the earth around him.

His position, however, became a blessing in disguise because the Germans had to raise their heads to see him, and each time they appeared he fired a deadly shot. Having grown up as a hunter, York possessed a remarkable ability with firearms. But with each clip of ammunition he used, his gun barrel grew hotter and hotter until he feared he might run out of bullets.

In a brave move, he stood up and continued his defense, when suddenly a German officer and five men charged at him with fixed bayonets. Using his hunting techniques, York downed the last man first and then the second from the last until he reached the leader. He then turned his attention back to the soldiers manning the machine guns.

136

Since he did not want to kill any more of the enemy than was absolutely necessary, he called to them asking for their surrender, but the Germans continued firing. York fired a few more rounds and addressed the Germans again.

Among the German prisoners who had been captured by surprise was a major. He offered to make the other Germans surrender if York would stop shooting. York agreed. When the German Major blew his whistle, the Germans came down the hill with hands raised high. Later, York examined the major's pistol, and, finding it empty, concluded that the major had been shooting at him from behind at some point in the battle. Among the surrendering Germans was one man who threw a hand grenade at York's head, but it missed him and hit a prisoner. A shot from York's pistol silenced the rebellious German.

ALVIN C. YORK

During the battle, York had killed no less than twenty-five Germans and had captured somewhere between eighty and ninety. The German line had been captured by only eight Americans, York and seven others.

Escorted by York and his men, and carrying the wounded Americans, the German prisoners made their way toward the Allied lines. As they went, they approached another German line, and York commanded them to surrender. One German refused to comply, and York was compelled to shoot him. Slowly, the eight Americans marched their 132 German prisoners to the American line. Arriving at Camp Headquarters, York handed the prisoners over to the military police. Brigadier General Lindsay greeted York, "Well, York, I hear you have captured the whole German army."

As a result of that day's battle, York was promoted to sergeant. A strong Christian, York knew it was Divine protection that had kept him safe. He later wrote, "I have been trying to figure it out ever since. And the more I figure the more I am convinced that it warsn't no mere luck or jes an accident. It must have been something more and bigger than that."

Alvin had not always been a devout, peace-loving man. Born on December 13, 1887, in Pall Mall, a little community in the Cumberland Mountains of Tennessee, he learned to appreciate the beauty of nature. Growing up in the undeveloped Valley of the Three Forks of the Wolf, York received very little education. He learned farming, plowing, blacksmithing, and marksmanship from his father. At many shooting matches, Alvin was the winning participant. During the war, his knowledge of guns and shooting proved very useful.

In 1911, York's father died, causing him to reject his Christian upbringing and enter a life of pleasure. He began drinking, gambling, swearing, and fighting. Earnestly, his little mother petitioned the Lord to change her wayward son, and she reminded Alvin of his good Christian father. As the seed of truth began to grow in his heart, he started to give up his bad habits, and on January 1, 1915, he turned his life over to Christ. Leaving his past behind, he never again returned to his wild life. York later admitted that it took more courage to surrender to Jesus than it did to capture Hill 223 during the war. York became a passionate soldier for Christ.

When the dedicated and God-fearing York received his draft notice, he appealed to the draft board as a conscientious objector. Since the only creed of the church York attended was the Bible, and the church held no official position against participation in war, York's plea was refused.

York's commitment to God guided his life, but so did his devotion to his country. Although it was a sad, homesick Alvin who arrived at Camp Gordon, Georgia, he made an excellent soldier and obeyed orders. In his heart he still believed "Thou shall not kill" applied even to war.

Praying fervently, he decided to discuss his views with his commanding officers, Captain Danforth and Major Buxton. They brought to light several things York had never considered, including the suffering of the people in Belgium and France. When they granted York ten days leave, he headed for his beloved hills of Tennessee to search for God's will. During his vacation, he spent a great deal of time studying God's Word and praying. He later wrote in his autobiography, "I knowed I would be protected from all harm. And that so long as I believed in Him He would not allow even a hair of my head to be harmed." York followed God's leading and went to war. The United States received the service of a mighty man of God when he captured Hill 223 in the Argonne Forest.

York's amazing feat made him an instant hero. He received the American Distinguished Service Cross and the

Congressional Medal of Honor, the highest decoration for bravery.

When the cease-fire was announced on November 11, 1918, York longed to go home to his mother and to his sweetheart, Gracie Williams. It was May 10, 1919, when the celebrated hero arrived in Pall Mall.

York followed his commanding officer, Jesus Christ, even when God asked him to do a difficult task, and his legacy continues even today.

Digging Deeper

What was the hill that York captured called?

How many Germans did York capture?

Locate Pall Mall, Tennessee, on an atlas.

Watch the movie *Sergeant York* starring Gary Cooper. This wonderful black and white classic does a remarkable job of retelling York's story.

Read *Sergeant York and the Great War* by Alvin C. York, available from Mantle Ministries. Although York lacked a good education, he did not let that stop him from writing his autobiography. Complete with misspellings and poor grammar, this book is a look at the real life of a great man. York shares about his life growing up in the backwoods of Tennessee, his conversion to Christ, his plea as a conscientious objector, and his participation in World War I.

Chapter 24

The Great Depression

Imagine that banks suddenly close, dissolving people's life savings, and all income is cut off. With very little money to spend on merchandise, more companies go out of business, and this makes the unemployment rate even higher. Just such a scenario really happened in the 1930s. It has become known as the Great Depression, perhaps one of the worst economic calamities in history. Its effects were felt not only in the United States, but also all over the world.

On October 29, 1929—a date that is remembered by the foreboding name of Black Tuesday—the stock market crashed. The value of stocks dropped $14 billion, an estimated 16,410,030 stocks were sold, and $30 billion was lost on that unfortunate day.

To fully understand the Great Depression and the stock market crash, a look at the 1920s is essential. After World War I, a great many changes took place in the American economy. Mass production made it easy for consumers to buy new inventions, such as cars, radios, refrigerators, and vacuum cleaners. These goods were seen as a necessity instead of a luxury, and people began purchasing them on credit, which led to debt. People also invested in risky business ventures called speculations. There were several different kinds of speculations, but one of the most popular was buying a portion of a bond and then using the bond as collateral to get a loan to pay for the rest of the bond. While the stock market was doing well, this was an easy way to make a profit, but when it crashed, many people lost everything they had.

The Roaring Twenties were a time of prosperity, but in October of 1929, the happy times ended. A vicious cycle began: banks closed, which caused sales to go down, and with fewer purchases, businesses closed, making the unemployment rate skyrocket.

Overnight, the United States went from a prosperous country to a poor one, and the man who received the blame was President Herbert Hoover. Someone must be responsible for the shattered economy, and therefore the president was held responsible. In an effort to lighten the severity of the situation, Hoover decided to call it a "depression" instead of a "panic" or "crisis" as other economic downturns had been named. Hoover did not believe in big government, so he waited for the economy to improve on its own. To help the American people, he cut taxes by one hundred and forty million dollars, and when things still didn't improve, he began programs to help the nation.

Unfortunately, the Hawley-Smoot Tariff, which raised tariff rates on thousands of imported goods, made Hoover even more unpopular. Trying to encourage Americans to buy products made in their own country, Hoover began taxing imported goods. The tariff had the opposite impact from the one Hoover intended, and it practically stopped all foreign trade.

The 1930s were a difficult time for the American people. In 1933, thirteen million people (twenty-five percent of the nation) were unemployed. In 1938 that number was ten million, and by 1939, nine million still remained without work.

The effects of the Great Depression varied from region to region. Some areas were hit hardest at the beginning, and others suffered most at the end. As the unemployed struggled to find jobs, the bread lines grew. Many chose to "ride the rails" looking for work. They were called hobos, and they rode in empty freight cars from one place to another, hoping to find employment. In 1932, the Pacific Railroad removed 650,000 trespassers from their trains. The Great Depression did not just touch a certain group; it affected the entire nation. Nearly everyone was poor or just getting by.

Despite the hard times (or maybe because of them), the American people found ways to make do with what they had. Adult clothes were made over for children. Wisely, people grew their own gardens and canned food for the winter. If anyone had a little extra, they were generous and shared it with others. People who had very little still helped others. Ingenious housewives would stretch the soup by adding water, and leaf salad might have celery leaves in it to make it go farther. Americans used their own common sense to make things last longer, and they found new uses for discarded things.

OKLAHOMA FAMILY ON THEIR WAY TO CALIFORNIA

Although the Depression wasn't Hoover's fault, the citizens of the United States elected Franklin Delano Roosevelt to replace him in the 1932 election. Roosevelt promised the people a New Deal, and shortly after taking office in 1933, he declared a bank holiday to evaluate which banks were sound. Nearly ninety-five percent of the banks reopened.

During the First Hundred Days, Roosevelt called a special session of Congress during which many of his New Deal programs were passed. No president before had ever attempted to drastically change the role of the American government as Roosevelt did. Until that time, caring for the poor had been the responsibility of private organizations, but Roosevelt made it the job of the government. His programs became known as Alphabet Soup because they were identified by their initials. There was the Agricultural Adjustment Act (AAA), the Civilian Conservation Corps (CCC), and the National Industrial Recovery Act (NIRA), just to mention a few. Some of these programs seemed very successful and gave the people hope for a better future, but some believed they were socialistic. For instance, the Supreme Court condemned the NIRA as unconstitutional in 1935. Although the Depression was still going strong in 1936, Roosevelt was reelected. The economy had another downturn in 1937. It was called Roosevelt's Recession. During the Great Depression, the role of the government changed drastically.

A severe drought on the Great Plains added more problems to the shaky economy. The Dust Bowl covered many states, but Oklahoma suffered the most. Over one thousand "Okies" left their homes and headed to California. During the First World War, farmers had turned pasture land into cultivated fields to help feed Europe and the troops. They did not practice crop rotation, depleting the soil of nutrients. With the decline in farming in the 1930s, the fields were used again for grazing. Unfortunately, when cattle returned to the land, they ground the dry dirt into a powdery soil. Dust storms even reached places like Washington D.C. After the Depression, farmers worked to improve their methods so the Dust Bowl years would never be repeated.

Even though times were hard, people enjoyed many forms of amusement. Radio programs delighted people of all ages. Movies were also a way to escape from the daily challenge of making do. In 1939, people went to see *Mr. Smith Goes to Washington, Gone With the Wind,* and *The Wizard of Oz.* Comic strips such as *Little Orphan Annie* and *Tarzan* were also very popular.

Throughout the 1930s, people found means of entertaining themselves by social gatherings. Children enjoyed playing with homemade kites and rag dolls and participating in other amusements like roller skating, baseball, kick the can, and taking a dip at the local swimming hole. Complaining was not normal during the 1930s. People just made the most of every situation.

The Great Depression finally ended when the United States entered World War II. On Sunday, December 7, 1941, the Japanese attacked Pearl Harbor. Producing equipment for the war now became a national effort.

The 1930s forged the American people into a strong, determined country. After facing over ten years of economic hardship, America was prepared to fight against egotistical tyrants. The Great Depression was a training ground that produced a hearty, industrious generation. No longer were they fighting against hunger, money problems, and joblessness. Their new enemies were Hitler, Mussolini, and Japan. People who lived through the hard times of the 1930s have a determination that can still be felt in this nation.

Digging Deeper

When did the Great Depression begin?

When did it end?

Make an outline of the events that happened during the Great Depression.

Read *When the Banks Closed, We Opened Our Hearts* from the readers of Reminisce Magazine. This book has pictures and stories from people who lived during the Great Depression.

Interview someone who lived during the Depression. It might be a grandparent or great-grandparent, a family member, or a friend. Ask them questions about life in the '30s. (For example: Did you know several people who were out of work? Did you meet a hobo? What were some ways that your family made do? Did anyone in your family work for one of Roosevelt's programs like the CCC?) After the interview, compile your information into a report.

Chapter 25

The Navajo Code Talkers

On April 18, 1943, a group of Japanese planes flew toward the Solomon Islands. Aboard one of the airplanes was the mastermind behind the attack on Pearl Harbor, Admiral Isoroku Yamamoto. Although the trip was slightly dangerous, it seemed impossible that the Allies could know the exact place and time of his arrival.

As Yamamoto's plane prepared to land, his escort pulled back. Suddenly, eighteen American P-38 Lightning aircraft appeared in the sky. The shocked escort tried to regroup, but the Americans delivered a deadly fire into Yamamoto's plane. It plummeted to the earth in flames. As quickly as they had appeared, the Americans headed for safety with barely enough fuel to reach their airfield.

This cleverly planned attack shows the significance of obtaining top-secret information from the enemy. During the early months of the Second World War, both the United States and Japan were able to crack every code the other nation created. It was clear that to win the war in the Pacific, an unbreakable code must be found so that closely guarded secrets would not fall into enemy hands.

While military personnel were working on the code problem, the solution was in the American southwest. Many years before, in the late 1800s, William and Margaret Johnston and their young son Philip served as missionaries to the Navajo. Philip was four at the time and learned the Navajo language by playing with the other children. After the Japanese attacked Pearl Harbor on December 7, 1941, Philip Johnston suggested using the Navajo language to create a code for the military. It was such a complex language that unless learned from infancy it was nearly impossible to master, and it was a verbal language only— no written version existed.

Because of the urgent need for concise methods of communication, General Clayton B. Vogel agreed to test Johnston's plan. In early 1942, Johnston and four Navajo volunteers arrived at Camp Elliott near San Diego to do a demonstration. It was a huge success.

The Marines decided the Navajo language could be used as a code, and they arranged for Johnston to organize the 382nd Platoon of the U.S. Marines. Originally the program called for 200 recruits, but it was cut back to a test program with just thirty men. Heading to the Navajo Reservation, the Marines looked for young men who were fluent in both English and Navajo.

The reservation was like an independent country within the United States. It was twenty-five thousand square miles—larger than West Virginia—and had been the home of the Navajo for hundreds of years. There were several government-run schools on the reservation. These schools sternly forbade the students from speaking Navajo. If the children were caught talking in the Navajo language, they had their mouths washed out with soap or were given demerits. In this strict atmosphere, Navajo children learned to speak English fluently. Their knowledge of both English and Navajo would be very useful during World War II.

Although the Navajo recruits' primary job would be radio communication, they went through the vigorous training of the Marines. The hearty Navajos passed the fitness training with ease but found the rigid military regulation difficult. After completing boot camp, the thirty Navajos were sent to Camp Pendleton, where they learned about field radios and created the Navajo Code. Rather than just communicating through Navajo, they used Navajo words to represent military terms. For example, bomb would be "a-ye-shi" which was the Navajo word for egg; ship was "toh-dineh-ih," which meant "sea force." They also created their own alphabet to spell words that did not have a code name. *A* was "wol-la-chee," the Navajo word for ant, and *B* was "shush" for bear.

To test the merit of the new program, the Navajo were put in a mock battle while they demonstrated how the code worked. The Navajo Code Talkers were a success. Of the original thirty who enlisted, twenty-nine finished the pilot program. They were called the First 29. Johnston was put in command of the program, and two of the First 29 returned to the reservation to get new recruits for the program. Somewhere between 350–420 Navajos served during World War II as Navajo Code Talkers.

Finally, the code was ready to be used in actual combat. The first Navajo Code Talkers were sent to Guadalcanal in the Japanese-controlled South Pacific. As the Marines maneuvered through the jungle, their only source of communication was their radios. The Navajos' most deadly weapon, the code, nearly proved fatal to the Talkers. When the Marines, who knew nothing of the secret code, heard a strange language on the radio, they assumed it was Japanese. Before full-fledged chaos reigned, the officers restored order.

Situations like this only fueled the officers' skepticism of the Navajo Code Talkers. Despite their personal danger, however, the Navajos transmitted messages with speed and accuracy. Back in California, the Navajo Code supervisors were working to expand the code to include more terms. In the end, they had eight hundred words in the code.

The Navajo Code Talkers demonstrated their worth when the allies attacked Rabaul in November of 1943. Rabaul was a Japanese port in a strategic location. A surprise attack seemed impossible because the Japanese were able to decode every message the Americans sent. Finally, the Marines loaned eleven Navajo Code Talkers to the Navy, and from then on the Japanese knew nothing of the United States' plans. Although the surprise assault did not dislodge the Japanese from Rabaul, the position was no longer a threat.

The warfare of codes and ciphers was as powerful a part of World War II as dive-bombers and submarines. Through decoding, the U.S. discovered Japan's plans to attack Midway on June 5–6, 1942. After Midway, the U.S. military began "island hopping," and finally the Navajo Code Talkers became the most trusted source of communications. They participated in the fiercest battles of the war and performed their valuable task in the most dangerous situations.

When the Marines landed on Tarawa, the Marshall Islands, the Mariana Islands, Saipan, and Guam, the Code Talkers were there—risking their lives on the front lines to ensure reliable communication between the commanders and the companies. As bullets whizzed by and soldiers fell, the Navajo Code Talkers transmitted pertinent information about enemy positions and requests for medical assistance and reinforcements. After the battle on Guam, Colonel Marlow Williams said that the Code Talkers "were invaluable throughout the assault on Guam." Finally, the U.S. had created a code that baffled the Japanese. As the Marines began to see the benefits of the Code Talkers, they refused to send messages any other way.

Next, the U.S. invaded Iwo Jima. This island fortress was defended by twenty-two thousand Japanese soldiers and had impressive defenses. Before the Marines landed, Allied planes had bombed the island for seventy-four days, but the Japanese defenses were still strong. In February 1945, the first wave of Marines landed. The Navajo Code Talkers were in the second group to reach Iwo Jima. After the beach was populated with Marines, the hidden Japanese began a deadly fire on the Americans. As the Marines moved forward to dislodge the Japanese, the Navajos were busy sending messages. During the first forty-eight hours of the assault on Iwo Jima, the Navajo Code Talkers sent and received eight hundred messages!

The gruesome fighting continued for over a month, and finally, on March 16, 1945, the Americans were victorious. It had been a costly battle—6,800 killed and 20,000 wounded. When the Marines planted the U.S. flag on Mount Suribachi, the Code Talkers transmitted the message. Major Howard Conner praised the Navajo for their service: "Were it not for the Navajo Code Talkers, the Marines never would have taken Iwo Jima."

On August 6, 1945, the United States dropped the first atomic bomb on Hiroshima. When Japan refused to surrender, the U.S. dropped another A-bomb, this time at Nagasaki on the ninth of August. This brought World War II to an end. Despite the end of hostilities, however, the Navajo were asked to keep the code a secret in case it was needed in another war. The code was used again in the Korean and Vietnam Conflicts.

Finally, in 1969, the brave men who created and used the only unbreakable code were awarded for their actions during the reunion of the Fourth Marine Division Association. August 14, 1982, was named National Code Talkers Day. The Navajo Code Talkers contribution to history was felt long before they received national acclaim.

Digging Deeper

Find the places mentioned in this chapter on a map.

Discuss what might have happened if Philip Johnston's family had not been missionaries to the Navajo and if there had never been a Navajo Code.

Use an encyclopedia or history book to create a time line of World War II events.

Read *Navajo Code Talkers* by Nathan Aaseng. This is a very informative book and has many pictures of the Code Talkers.

Visit this Web site to see the Navajo Code:
http://www.history.navy.mil/faqs/faq61-4.htm.

Bonus Chapters

~

A Tribute to Famous Mothers
The Hand That Rocks the Cradle

~

Explorers
Medieval Explorer Marco Polo

Evangelistic Explorer David Livingston

Daring Explorer of Antarctica Robert Falcon Scott

~

Uncover Exciting History

Bonus Chapter 1

The Hand That Rocks the Cradle
Mothers Who Changed the
World Through Their Children

Mother—what a wonderful name! The very sound of it brings visions of love and tenderness. Motherhood is the oldest and one of the most worthy professions of women. Since the beginning of time, noble and virtuous women have given the world brave and heroic sons and daughters who learned the way of truth from their mothers. These women are the unsung heroes of the world, but in their own hearts, they only wished for their children to reflect the love of God. In their own quiet way, these ladies changed the world.

WASHINGTON   LINCOLN   GARFIELD

Mother of Augustine

Not far from the ancient and magnificent city of Carthage was a small town called Thagaste. In this village lived a virtuous Christian named Monica. Tragically, this righteous woman was married to a pagan named Patricius, and when they had a son, Augustine, on November 13, 354 A.D., her husband refused to allow her to teach the boy about Christ. Praying fervently, she watched as her son grew into a young man. She once sought the advice of a Christian teacher who told her, "Go thy way, go thy way and God help thee; it is not possible that the child of these tears should perish."

While Augustine was still a youth, Patricius died, but Augustine had already begun living a sinful life. During his education in Carthage, he broke his precious mother's heart by his wild living. In 373, he began his career as an instructor of rhetoric and years later taught in Milan. It was in Milan that he met a Christian as devout and righteous as his mother, the Bishop Ambrose. Slowly, the power of God's salvation began to seep into his life.

On Easter Sunday in 387 A.D., a faithful mother watched her precious son be baptized and commit his life to her Lord, Jesus Christ. Monica's sinning son became a leading Christian.

Augustine praised his mother with these words: "It was owing to the faithful and daily prayers of my mother that I did not perish." At the age of fifty-six, Monica went to her eternal home happy with the knowledge that one day her son would join her. Augustine went on to become the Bishop of Hippo, an influential preacher, and one of the most well-known writers of the early church. Powerful are the prayers of a Christian mother!

Mother of Abraham Lincoln

When looking at great men, it is always interesting to learn about their mothers. It is only natural that skillful women should have notable sons. Such was the case with Nancy Hanks Lincoln. Virginia was the birthplace of this impressive lady. At the age of twelve, she went to live with her uncle and aunt, Thomas and Elizabeth Sparrow. They provided her with a thorough education, and she learned the art of fine needlework and became a skilled seamstress. Creating wedding clothes and other finery, Nancy earned an outstanding reputation for her work.

At the age of twenty-two, Nancy met a man named Thomas Lincoln. On June 12, 1806, in the backwoods of Kentucky, a tall, attractive, honest-faced Nancy Hanks married a well-built, handsome Thomas Lincoln. A small cabin in Elizabethtown was their first home. Later, unexpectedly, Thomas moved them to Hardin County, Kentucky.

In a rugged log cabin on February 12, 1809, Nancy gave birth to her second child, Abraham Lincoln. Being a resourceful, loving woman, Nancy was troubled by her husband's lazy, slothful ways. He moved his family often, always hoping to improve their circumstances and never realizing it was his own neglect that caused their hardships. Quietly, Nancy endured the harsh existence of backwoods life and found joy in Abraham's keen desire for knowledge. Abraham turned to his kind mother for understanding and comfort, but stayed away from his harsh father.

Nancy's body had been weakened by years of hard living, and she succumbed to an epidemic called milk sickness on October 5, 1818. Years after her death, Abraham Lincoln said of his influential mother, "All that I am or hope to be I owe to my angel mother."

Stepmother of Abraham Lincoln

Abraham Lincoln's stepmother proved to be as great a blessing to him as his own mother. Sarah Bush, a widow with three children of her own, agreed to marry Thomas Lincoln when he proposed. When Sarah first saw Thomas

Lincoln's children, her motherly heart reached out to the unkempt children. Quickly she transformed the forlorn, dirty cabin into a spotless home. Then she began to provide the children with an education. Seeing Abe's keen mind, Sarah encouraged him to read and broaden his knowledge, which Thomas thought was nonsense.

Sarah loved the Lincoln children as her own. After Thomas died in 1851, Abraham provided for his stepmother as if he was her natural son. Sarah Bush Lincoln lived to see Abraham elected to the highest office in the land. Through her encouragement, he had survived his troubled childhood and gone on to greatness. Sarah once said of him, "I can say what not one mother in a thousand can say, Abraham never gave me one hard word." Abraham said of her, "She proved to be a good and kind mother." Taking the time to love a motherless boy, Sarah in her own way affected history.

Mother of James A. Garfield

Another amazing mother of a president was Eliza Ballou Garfield. In 1801, Eliza was born in the state of New Hampshire. Being from a religious and righteous family, she demonstrated a life devoted to both Christ and virtue. She grew up in the state of New York, and it was there that she married Abram Garfield. In the true pioneer spirit, Abram moved his family to the Ohio wilderness. Courageously, they cleared trees, planted crops, and built a cabin, where their fourth child, James Abram Garfield, was born. (He was the last president to be born in a log cabin.) Enjoying life, the Garfield family endured their hard work with cheerfulness.

Unexpectedly, life changed for Eliza and her four children when Abram died. Many friends suggested that she sell her farm and go back east, but the determined woman decided to raise her children on the farm her husband had built.

If one word could be used to describe Eliza, it would be self-sacrifice. She and the children worked endlessly to provide for themselves. Through her example, she taught them to serve the Lord, work hard, and live honestly. Many years later, when Eliza was called Grandmother Garfield, she stood at her son's inaugural address. After taking the oath of office, the new president kissed the Holy Bible and then leaned down to his own sweet mother and kissed her. What a beautiful tribute of thankfulness to a self-sacrificing mother!

Mother of George Washington

What kind of mother did George Washington have? Mary Ball was such a good-natured girl while growing up in the colony of Virginia that she was called "Sweet Molly Ball." Although she received only a meager education, she learned the essential skills of sewing, cleaning, and running a household. Mary's widowed mother instructed her in the Christian walk, and Mary held firmly to Jesus all her life.

In 1731, Mary Ball married widower Augustine Washington. A year later, on February 22, 1732, God blessed them with a son, George Washington. Faithfully, Mary and her husband held family worship each morning and evening. After twelve years of happily married life, Augustine died, leaving a large family for Mary to raise.

Facing many cares, Mary overcame them with diligence. In gentleness and love, she imparted to the children the importance of obedience and duty. Slowly, one by one, her children grew into adults. When George received the commission to lead the American troops in the Revolutionary War, he visited his mother before departing. The righteous lady prayed God's blessing on his life and then said, "Go my son, and do your duty."

Many were the requests Mary brought before the Lord during the following years. George again visited his dear mother before filling the role as the first United States president. This meeting was their last, for Mary Ball Washington died shortly afterward at the age of eighty-five. She once remarked, "I am not surprised at what George has done, for he was always a very *good* boy." Mary invested godly character into her children and received the blessing of seeing them live by God's standards.

Mother of John and Charles Wesley

If education begins at home, then John and Charles Wesley had an excellent start, thanks to the insight and instruction of their mother. In the city of London, during the year of 1669 or 1670, Susanna Annesley entered the world. Receiving a remarkable education from her father, Susanna was thoroughly trained in Greek, Latin, Logic, and Mathematics. When she was a blooming youth, she met a minister named Samuel Wesley. They married in 1690. During their long, happy years together, God blessed them with many children.

Besides being a faithful wife and mother, Susanna was also responsible for her children's education. She said, "I insist upon conquering the will of children early, because this is the only strong and rational foundation of a religious education, without which both precept and example will be ineffectual." Six hours of each day were devoted to learning. Through her gentleness and patience, the children received an excellent education. The religious and scholarly training the Wesley children obtained from their mother never left them. And when they were grown, they praised her for her virtue.

Each of these women radiated the three essential characteristics that make a good mother—devotion to God, dedication to His will, and diligence in His work. It has often been said, "The hand that rocks the cradle rules the world." How true that is!

Digging Deeper

Read *Mothers of Famous Men* from Lamplighter
Publishing. This is a fabulous book that has many short
sketches of influential mothers.

Write a short biography in honor of your own mother. Fill
it with all the wonderful things she has done for you and
others.

In an encyclopedia, look up the men mentioned in this
chapter and read about their many accomplishments.

On a map, locate the different geographical places
mentioned in this chapter.

Bonus Chapter 2

Medieval Explorer
Marco Polo

Marco Polo of Venice was a great medieval explorer. Sometime during the 1200s, his father, Nicolas Polo, and his uncle, Maffeo Polo, had traveled to China to establish trade. Finding great favor with the Khan of China, the brothers were commissioned by him to go to the Pope at Rome and bring back people who could tell the Khan more about the Christian religion.

When Nicolas and Maffeo returned to Europe, they found that Pope Clement IV had died, and a successor had not yet been named. The Polo brothers delayed their journey as long as possible, but at length they departed for China, this time taking the young man Marco Polo with them. After traveling for three and a half years, they finally arrived in China. Their journey took them over deserts, mountains, rivers, and strange lands. The Polo family experienced the exotic novelties of the unknown East.

The Polos' trek began in 1271 when they voyaged to Acre on the east side of the Mediterranean Sea. Next, they sailed to Armenia. Then they began an extraordinary land journey along the Silk Road to the Far East. Briskly, they traveled through Persia with its arid deserts and refreshing oases. At the Plain of Pamier, the high elevation and great cold made the passage across the arid mountains extremely unpleasant. Next they came to the Great Desert (now called the Gobi Desert), with its hills and valleys of sand. There was no vegetation, but they did find fresh water scattered throughout the vast desert. Journeying through the barren wilderness, rugged mountains, and pleasant plains, the Polos eventually reached their destination, Shangtu, in the present-day country of China.

The ruler of the country of Cathay (China) was Kublai Khan. He was the grandson of Genghis Khan, the Mongols' heroic leader, who had conquered much of Asia and had established the Tartar (Mongol) people as supreme leaders. Kublai Khan's capital city was called Cambaluc, or Cathay, the present-day city of Beijing.

Inside the capital, the Great Khan had a magnificent palace that was so large it covered four square miles. The inside walls were overlaid with gold and silver, and there was a dining hall that could hold six thousand people. Kublai Khan also had another palace in Shangtu that was made of marble with walls that were adorned by exquisite paintings of animals and humans. The complete area of the palace was sixteen square miles.

Being fond of hunting, Kublai Khan had over five hundred hawks and similar birds that he used for pursuing game, as well as leopards and tigers that were trained to chase boars, wild cattle, bears, and donkeys for the purpose of aiding a hunter. Another strange sight that the Europeans saw was paper money. Making paper from the bark of trees, the Tartars then added the seal of the Great Khan, which made the paper money official. The paper money was always backed by gold or silver, so it retained its value.

To help improve the trade of his capital city, Kublai Khan had a broad, deep channel dug between it and the city of Kwa-chau. The waterway, which was equivalent to a great river, allowed large vessels to make the voyage to the capital city. Because the Khan was very interested in what took place in his kingdom, he also had an extensive message carrier system which was very similar to the American Pony Express of the 1800s. Every twenty or thirty miles in Cathay there was a station that had four hundred horses, with two hundred horses always in readiness to carry the Khan's messages. This express kept Kublai Khan well informed and allowed him to send important communications and orders quickly. Kublai Khan was a great ruler!

On their travels, and during their years in Cathay, the Polos saw and heard of many natural wonders. They were told of a place where natural oil springs occurred. The natives collected and burned the oil to create heat. In another area, the inhabitants used steel to make mirrors. Crossing the harsh deserts of Asia, the Tartars sustained themselves on dried milk that they added to water. The Europeans were amazed! Stranger still, the people had black stones that burned. The black stones, which were undoubtedly coal, created effective heat.

The abundant wealth of the East was incredible. They had gold, silver, and other metals and precious stones such as azure, pearls, turquoise, diamonds, and rubies. There were also exotic spices and seasonings such as cinnamon, ginger, sugar, and pepper. Asia certainly contained many marvels.

Marco Polo so impressed the Great Khan by his prudence and thoroughness that the Khan employed him as an ambassador. Industriously, Marco learned several different languages. While attending to the Khan's affairs, Marco discovered many of the natural and man-made wonders of Cathay. Journeying to the south and southwest of Cathay, Marco saw the fertile land of the Huang He River (or Yellow River), so named because of its yellowish color. The Huang He River was so wide that a bridge could not be constructed across it, and the river's depths were astounding. Because of the river, the land around it was very productive.

On the Khan's business, Marco traveled to many other cities, one of which was Su-chau, a very noble city with six thousand large bridges that ships could pass under. Among the mountain peaks of that area, the inhabitants grew large amounts of ginger and rhubarb. Marco Polo also became the governor of a city called Yang-chau. He held that post for three years, to the delight of Kublai Khan.

After many years the Polos wished to return to Venice. Kublai Khan was getting old, and the other members of his court were jealous of the position that the Polo family had. Marco, his father, and his uncle were uncertain about what would happen to them when the Khan died, but Kublai Khan loathed parting with them. Finally, they persuaded the Khan to let them depart, and they formed part of an escort for a bride that was being taken to a king in Levant.

Their homeward journey was by way of the sea, a welcome alternative to the dreadful land trek they had made coming to Cathay. Traveling from the China Sea through the Strait of Malacca, the Polo family stopped at Ceylon, now called Sri Lanka. The lovely island with its coastal plains and forested mountains was a place of abundant wealth, with amethyst, topaz, sapphires, and an enormous ruby that was the size of the palm of a human hand, as thick as a man's arm, and the color of fire.

After twenty-six years' absence the Polos returned to the thriving merchant town of Venice. Although they were very wealthy men, they had a difficult time convincing their fellow citizens that they were indeed Nicolas, Maffeo, and Marco Polo. Their friends, however, finally believed the Polos!

In a war between Venice and their rival city of Genoa, Marco Polo was captured and put in prison. During his imprisonment, Marco dictated his adventures and travels to a fellow prisoner, Rusticiano of Pisa. The book that resulted, *A Description of the World,* became very influential and inspired other explorers who were interested in finding a sea route to the Orient. One of those explorers was Christopher Columbus, who braved the unknown Atlantic Ocean looking for a quicker way to the fortunes of the East that Marco Polo wrote about in his book. Instead, Columbus stumbled across a whole new continent. Marco Polo had a great impact on history and the world by opening people's minds to unknown places and people.

Digging Deeper

Where was Marco Polo from?

What influence did Polo's book have on the world?

What was China called in the Middle Ages?

Who were the Tartars?

Read *Marco Polo and the Medieval Explorers* by Rebecca Stefoff. This book is a good overview of the life of Marco Polo and world events during the 1200s.

Other subjects to study: Genghis Khan, Kublai Khan, the Gobi Desert, Venice, the Silk Road.

Look in a world history book or a time line and see what world events were happening during the late 1200s.

Learn about falcons and how they have been historically used for hunting.

Study how the Mongols dressed (a costume book on Asian dress would be a good resource), how they made a living, their customs, their manner of warfare (look in an encyclopedia), and their homes (look in an encyclopedia under "yurts," then try building a miniature yurt using Popsicle sticks and cover it with felt or fabric).

Find a Chinese cookbook and prepare a Chinese dinner. Then, if you want to add extra authenticity, eat the meal on a coffee table or other low table and have everyone sit on rugs and recline on cushions or pillows in true Chinese style.

Bonus Chapter 3

Evangelistic Explorer
David Livingstone

Rarely does one find an explorer who had the character and virtue that Dr. David Livingstone possessed. Many explorers achieved worthy accomplishments in their work, but sadly many of them did not have heroic character in their daily lives. Livingstone, however, in addition to his great accomplishments, was also a Christian and lived it out in his every activity. He viewed his main purpose in life to be that of an evangelist, and he shared the gospel wherever he went.

Born on March 19, 1813, in Blantyre, Scotland, David Livingstone was raised in a godly home. His relaxed childhood was shortened when at the tender age of ten he went to work at a factory. From six in the morning till eight at night he toiled at the factory. Many times he would bring a book and catch a few sentences when time allowed.

At the age of nineteen, he enrolled at the Glasgow University with the intent of becoming a doctor, while inwardly he felt God calling him to do missionary work. He applied to the London Missionary Society for support. After graduating in 1840, he made preparations to go to

China, but the Opium War prevented him. God opened up a door to Africa, and David willingly went.

Dr. Livingstone's first years in Africa were very informative. He made his home among the natives and learned much about how they lived. He also found the diverse land in southern Africa very fascinating. Being interested in the African animals, he once had a terrifying encounter with a ferocious lion. The lion had been causing disturbances among the tribes, so Livingstone joined a group of men to search for the animal. While they were hunting, the lion appeared. David shot both barrels of his gun, but the animal still attacked him. The mauling seriously injured David's left shoulder and arm. He was taken to the home of Robert Moffat, where he was nursed back to health by Dr. Moffat's daughter, Mary. A relationship grew between David and Mary, and they were married in 1844. His first years in Africa were enlightening, but he had not yet begun his most memorable work.

Why did Dr. Livingstone become an explorer? He wanted to share the Good News with people who had never heard it. His first taste of exploring came when he journeyed north from his missionary station at Kuruman and through the Kalahari Desert with its trackless plains and prairie grass. This trip was made again in 1849. In August of that year, Livingstone reached Lake Ngami, becoming the first recorded white man to see it. Finding Lake Ngami was an important discovery.

As the expedition continued, Livingstone came down with malaria. Throughout his life, he suffered severely from various kinds of diseases, but he never let them stop him. He kept pressing on with the bold perseverance of a true Christian and a determined explorer.

He did so many noteworthy things as an explorer that it is easy to forget that he was also an evangelist. Unlike other whites, he lived among the natives, thus sharing in their lives in a very special way. Certainly his most important mission was to spread the gospel. He lived what he preached.

He also showed his genuine concern for the Africans by openly opposing slavery. Even during the mid-1800s, the barbaric practice of slavery was still a driving force in Africa. Dr. Livingstone hated slavery! On at least one occasion, he drove away some slave catchers and set free those who were in chains. Sadly, many of the trails he opened up were used by slave catchers. Nothing grieved Dr. Livingstone more than having his explorations used to exploit the natives.

During the years of 1852–1853, Dr. Livingstone led another expedition. After traveling through the Kalahari Desert, he reached the Chobe River, whose banks were surrounded by a dense forest. Paddling down the river in canoes, he and his men encountered numerous kinds of water snakes. Eventually they reached Linyanti, a town of the Makolol tribe. Livingstone hoped to find a suitable location for a missionary station, but when he became ill with malaria, the spot was considered unhealthy and they continued their trip.

In his own words, he explained what he intended to do next: "I shall open up a path to the interior or perish, I never have had the shadow of a shade of doubt as to the propriety of my course." Departing from Linyanti on November 11, 1853, they followed a northwesterly route. They arrived at the coastal city of Luanda on May 3, 1854. In only six and a half months, the exploration crew had traveled fourteen hundred miles.

Dr. Livingstone journeyed back across the continent because he had promised the men who came to Luanda with him that he would take them home. Although he was urged to go to England for a rest, he did his duty instead, which saved his life. Sadly, the boat that would have taken

171

him to England sank in the Atlantic Ocean with only one survivor. God was watching over Dr. Livingstone.

While traveling through the hostile country of the Chiboque tribe, Livingstone became ill with rheumatic fever, but with the Lord's help he persevered. While fording the Lotembwa River, he made one of his greatest geographical discoveries. According to his journals, he discovered the divide that separated rivers flowing south from those flowing north. Next he traveled east, eventually going through present-day Zimbabwe, Zambia, and Mozambique. Rumors had reached him of a tremendous waterfall, and Livingstone intended to find it. What he discovered was a massive falls that was 1,800 yards wide and descended 350 feet. It was a grand sight! The natives' name for the waterfall meant "smoke that thunders," but Livingstone called it Victoria Falls in honor of the Queen of England. When Livingstone reached the city of Quelimane on the east coast of Africa, he sailed for England to enjoy a much-deserved rest after all his travels.

STANLEY GREETING LIVINGSTONE

Dr. Livingstone's last expedition began in 1865 when he left England. The source of the Nile had always fascinated him, so he set out to locate it. Since the natives said it flowed out of a large lake in central Africa, Livingstone traveled extensively in Zaire, Zambia, and Tanzania. Days turned into months and months into years, and the outside world began to wonder if Livingstone was still alive. Newspaperman Henry Morton Stanley was given the assignment of finding Livingstone.

For two years Stanley searched for the lost missionary-explorer. Finally, on October 28, 1871, Stanley found Livingstone at Ujiji, on the banks of Lake Tanganyika. He greeted him with the now famous words, "Dr. Livingstone, I presume?"

Although Livingstone continued to explore, he did not have many more years to live. He died on May 4, 1873. His devoted friends buried his heart in Africa and embalmed his body, then they carried his remains to the coast, and Livingstone found his final rest at Westminster Abbey. His last journey had ended.

Dr. David Livingstone was a heroic man. When thinking of explorers in Africa, Dr. Livingstone inevitably comes to mind. During his life he traveled twenty-nine thousand miles in Africa, and most significantly, he unlocked one million square miles to the rest of the world. His drive for discovery opened up many trails into the continent, which were used by missionaries. Although he did not find the source of the Nile River, his contribution to the knowledge of Africa's geography is astounding. He also did many worthy things in the capacity of a missionary. He was an amazing explorer and an excellent evangelist.

Digging Deeper

Locate these places on an African map: Lake Ngami, Luanda, Victoria Falls, Quelimane, Nile River, Lake Tanganyika, Ujiji.

Spreading the gospel was Livingstone's main goal in life. Missionary work is still continuing in Africa. Do you know a missionary in Africa? Study about the country where they live. After you have done a little research about their country, send them a note of encouragement. (If you do not know a missionary in Africa, choose one African country to study.)

Study about the continent of Africa in an encyclopedia. Answer the following questions: How many square miles are in Africa? What are the main geographical features of Africa? Where is the highest point? Name some animals that are native to Africa. What is the largest lake? What is the longest river?

Read the book *David Livingstone: A Man of Prayer and Action* by C. Silvester Horne, M.P., a good book about the life and work of Livingstone.

Find some pictures of Victoria Falls either in an encyclopedia or a geography book. It truly is a magnificent sight.

Bonus Chapter 4

Daring Explorer of Antarctica
Robert Falcon Scott

When you think of explorers, what characteristics come to mind? Were they brave men who faced enormous obstacles to open up new land, or adventurous individuals who longed to discover unknown territory? Most explorers were proclaimed heroes by their countrymen. Yet how often do we hear the stories of men who perished while trying to achieve their goals of discovery? Robert Falcon Scott was a man with a dream. He had a sense of duty. He was determined to succeed. Unfortunately, this explorer's story did not end as he had planned.

Robert Falcon Scott was born on June 6, 1868, to John and Hannah Scott. Raised at Outlands, the family's home near Devonport, England, Scott enjoyed playing with his five siblings. Their mother, Hannah, was a pious Christian woman and a tender mother. At the young age of thirteen, Robert, commonly called Con, joined Her Majesty's Navy as a cadet. Over the next ten years, he rose to the rank of lieutenant and eventually became a torpedo lieutenant.

Being a devoted son, Con helped support his beloved mother after the death of her husband and a son, Archie. In between his expeditions, Con met and married Kathleen Bruce, a sculptress from London. Their lives were united on September 2, 1908, and they had one son.

Scott met a man in 1887 who changed his life. The man's name was Sir Clements Markham, a geographer who was interested in Antarctic exploration. Since Scott had won a race in the ship's dinghy, the captain honored him by inviting him to dinner. It was at this meal that Scott was first introduced to Sir Clements. Strangely, Markham decided from this one meeting that Scott was the right man to lead an expedition. Scott received an official letter of appointment from the Royal Geographic Society in 1900 asking him to lead a party of discovery to Antarctica. As Scott prepared for the journey to the mysterious south, he thought about the unexpected change that had come into his life.

MIDNIGHT SUN IN ANTARCTICA

In the summer of 1901, Scott and forty-seven men began their journey to Antarctica. Sailing aboard the *Discovery*, the men thought of the frigidly cold continent at the bottom of the world that was their destination. Land was sighted in December. As they charted the coastline, they kept a look out for a prospective place to set up a winter camp. While sailing east of the Ross Sea, they discovered a new land.

Scott named it King Edward VII Land in honor of the king of England. They chose a site for their camp on McMurdo Sound in February, 1902. Scott and another man took a trip in a hot air balloon that had been brought along to give the group an aerial view of Antarctica. Regrettably, the balloon began leaking and was only used once.

In November, Robert Scott, Dr. Edward Wilson, and Ernest Shackleton, who would later become a renowned explorer, began an extraordinary land trek south over the frozen continent. Their hope was to reach the South Pole. Day after day, the three men with their Siberian dogs and sledges traveled through the harsh white wilderness. Scott meticulously mapped the land they journeyed through. Eventually they had to turn back, even though the Pole had not been conquered.

As they continued the journey back to camp, they faced many difficulties: their rations began to run out, Shackleton suffered from scurvy, the blowing snow made their faces and lips dry and parched, and the sun's glare on the snow caused debilitating snow blindness. They finally arrived at their camp on February 3, 1903. Another year was spent in Antarctica because the *Discovery* was surrounded by ice. In January, 1904, the ship was released from the ice with the help of dynamite and sailed back to England. Scott had traveled three hundred miles south into the interior of Antarctica, the farthest any man had gone. He was welcomed home as a hero.

Scott began his second expedition in 1910 with the plan of being the first man to reach the South Pole. They again made their base camp at McMurdo Sound. From the start, things went badly. A motorized sledge that had been brought along broke through thin ice and was lost. Scott had decided to use ponies to pull the sledges, but the animals were too heavy, and they sank in the snow.

Sadly, the ship *Terra Nova* brought depressing news: the Norwegian Roald Amundsen and his expedition were encamped at the Bay of Whales, making preparations to conquer the South Pole ahead of the British and claim the honor of being the first to set foot on the South Pole. The race to the South Pole began!

Scott and his men set out. The support party left supplies of food, oil for heat, and other essentials along the way at logical places to be used by Scott and the four men who were going to the Pole on their return trip. As the support group headed back to the base camp, Scott and his band started the grueling journey to the South Pole. They endured high winds and slippery ground, continually pressing on to reach the Pole before the Norwegians.

On January 18, 1912, Scott and his group arrived at the long sought-after position of the South Pole, only to discover the flag of Norway nobly rippling in the wind. Roald Amundsen had accomplished his journey to the Pole a full month before. He left a tent that contained a letter for Scott and a letter for the King of Norway in case his expedition did not make it. Bitterly disappointed, Scott and his men raised the British flag and took a photograph, then quickly left the place that was now very hateful to them.

On the return trip, they found a fossilized rock that had the imprint of a leaf and stem, showing them that Antarctica had once been a place of vegetation. Cold weather and frequent storms delayed their journey. It took them longer to reach the depots of supplies than anticipated, and when they did get to them, they found the fuel oil cans had leaked. The men began to suffer from frostbite. One man died, and another wandered away, knowing he was holding back the progress of the party.

Only ten miles from the next depots, a roaring blizzard halted their progress. The prospects looked grim. They had only enough heat to cook one last meal. They were tired and sick. One of Scott's last journal entries said, "Had we lived I should have had a tale to tell of the hardihood, endurance, and courage of my companions which would have stirred the heart of every Englishman. These rough notes and our dead bodies must tell the tale." Scott and his two companions were found in November, 1912, by a search party. The second and last expedition of a brave man had ended.

Although Scott's life ended sadly, he would always be remembered for his contribution to the discoveries in Antarctica. His maps and expeditions paved the way for future explorations into the mysterious south. Scott was always driven by a deep sense of duty. As his widow Kathleen said, "There never was a man with such a sense of responsibility and duty, and the agony of leaving his job undone, losing the others' lives and leaving me uncared for must have been unspeakable." After Scott and his men had been found, the search party held a burial service. At the end the men sang Scott's favorite hymn, "Onward Christian Soldiers" a fitting anthem for a daring explorer.

DR. EDWARD WILSON

Digging Deeper

Look up the definition of *depots*.

Read about Antarctica in an encyclopedia or geography book and answer the following questions: How large is Antarctica? What does the word *Antarctica* mean? What is Antarctica's highest peak?

Who was the first man to reach the South Pole?

Name the cheerful-looking black and white birds that live on Antarctica.

Discuss the fact that the South Pole is really only the place where the invisible axis of the earth exists. In truth there is not a pole there at all.

Look on a map and find the South Pole, Ross Sea, Bay of Whales, and McMurdo Sound.

Read the book *Robert Falcon Scott* by Joan Bristow, a good overview of the explorer's life.

When the snow covers the ground this winter, set up a tent in your backyard and spend a day living like the Antarctic explorers. Cook lunch over a camp stove, go out exploring (perhaps a walk to the park), and keep a journal. Discuss what it would be like to live like this for months.

Index

Author Biography

Amy Puetz (pronounced Pitts) is a homeschool graduate, a self-taught historian, and a servant of Jesus Christ. History has been a passion for her since childhood. Years of in-depth study (both in modern and old sources) have equipped her to write history-related books. She especially loves to dig for little-known stories that show God's providential hand. Because of a chronic illness (fibromyalgia) that limits what she can do, the Lord led her to start an online business which she can do from home. She is the author of several e-books. In her spare time she enjoys sewing and reading. Visit her Web site at www.AmyPuetz.com to see many resources relating to history. She also publishes a bimonthly e-zine for ladies of all ages called, *Heroines of the Past.*

Other Books by Amy Puetz

Countdown to Christmas
Memory Making Stories and Activities for
Every Day from December 1st to the 25th

Imagine your family gathering each day to read a Christmas story and then participating in a fun activity. Make this a reality this holiday with *Countdown to Christmas*. The book is broken up into daily sections. Each day has a story and an activity that should take about thirty to forty-five minutes to go through. There are classic stories by well-known authors, such as Louisa May Alcott and Hans Christian Andersen to mention a few. This book has many different activities including games, crafts, cooking, riddles, quizzes, and singing carols. *Countdown to Christmas* will appeal to a large age group, but children from six to fourteen will probably enjoy it the most. This book has a mission to help families grow closer together.

Available at www.AmyPuetz.com

Other Books by Amy Puetz

Costumes With Character
Make Your Own Costumes from 11 Time Periods with 1 Dress!
Foreword by Mrs. Jennie Chancey

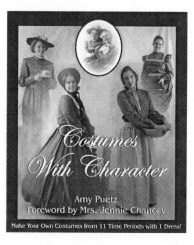

This exciting historical costume book has eleven creative costume patterns from the 1620s to the turn of the twentieth century (including Pilgrim, Puritan, Quaker, Revolutionary War, 1830s Pioneer, Civil War, two Victorian chapters, Turn of the Twentieth Century, and Sailor outfits), beautiful color photos, step-by-step easy-to-follow instructions, interesting facts about each time period, thought-provoking quotes by famous people, and a recommended resource reference chapter for further study.

"Amy's book made me excited about historical costumes again—costumes that I can easily make! I loved the simple instructions and helpful pictures."
~Nicole, age 16

Available at www.AmyPuetz.com

E-books by Amy Puetz

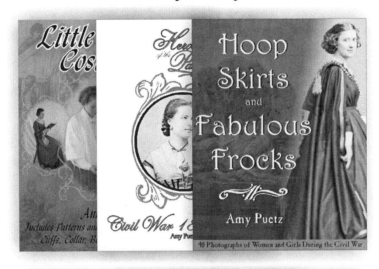

"I really enjoy your contributions to holding onto the part of the past that desperately needs to be a part of our present." ~Jill, homeschool mom

Available at www.AmyPuetz.com

LaVergne, TN USA
05 March 2010
175116LV00001B/242/P